"Propelled by Davis's sassy, confident voice and Kettner's energetic art, *Ink in Water* is a brave comic memoir of self-help and recovery. An uplifting true story, *Ink in Water* takes the reader through Davis's harrowing struggle with eating disorders and out the other side to where 'hope spreads too.' *Ink in Water* is about many things: punk rock mixtapes, vegan milkshakes, locked doors, 12-step meetings, and 'putting your faith in something that doesn't totally make sense.' *And* it's an adorable love story, told by an extraordinary husband-and-wife creative team."

—**Josh Neufeld**, writer/artist of *A.D.: New Orleans After the Deluge*

"In *Ink in Water*, Lacy Davis and Jim Kettner tell a cautionary tale of how little armor punk-feminist politics provide against a self-destroying eating disorder…when those politics are not underpinned by truly knowing one's own strength. For Lacy, it took a long, dark passage through feeling completely powerless—over herself and over her disease—and then, with the help of two crucial relationships, finding her own power deep inside to make her way out again. Kettner's fluid, expressive, energetic artwork is a perfect vehicle for this journey: he draws Lacy's pain—and her power—into every line in the book."

—**Jessica Abel**, author of *Growing Gills*, *Out on the Wire*, *La Perdida*, *Trish Trash*, and coauthor of *Drawing Words and Writing Pictures*

"*Ink in Water* is the candid and harrowing story of how young punk-feminist Lacy Davis won her life back from the jaws of an eating disorder. Artist Jim Kettner imbues each page with rich graytones, beautiful compositions, and characters so vivid, you could swear they were breathing. I recommend this to anyone with a body. It is a brave, beautiful, and important book."

—**Nicole J. Georges**, author of the graphic novels *Calling Dr. Laura* and *Fetch*

"Lacy Davis's candid writing style pulls you right into her personal journey. Kettner uses the comics medium beautifully to amplify Davis's powerful story. Davis and Kettner don't sugarcoat the serious effects of the eating disorder, yet manage to make the story very enjoyable to read. I read the entire book in one sitting. *Ink in Water* would give hope to anyone who is struggling with his or her inner demon."

—**Robin Ha**, author and illustrator for the *New York Times* bestseller, *Cook Korean!*

"Lacy Davis and Jim Kettner are newcomers to the graphic novel scene, but *Ink in Water* will definitely make them a household name. An incredibly important, extremely relatable memoir about learning to love the hardest person of all: yourself."

—**Liz Prince**, author of *Tomboy*, *Alone Forever*, and *Will You Still Love Me If I Wet The Bed*

INK IN WATER

an illustrated memoir

...OR, HOW I KICKED ANOREXIA'S ASS & EMBRACED BODY POSITIVITY!

BY

LACY J. DAVIS & JIM KETTNER

NEW HARBINGER PUBLICATIONS, INC.

PIP

PLIP

PIP

PLOP

plip
pip
pip
pip

FOR GALINA.

plip

Plop

plip

plip

plip

PLoP

PROLOGUE

PLOP

PLOP

PLOP!
SHIT!
SHIT!
SHIT...
PLOP!
PLOP!
PLOP!

PORTLAND, OREGON, 2010

Bethany Lutheran Church

GOD PREFERS KIND
ATHEISTS OVER
HATEFUL CHRISTIANS

EVERY MEETING STARTED
EXACTLY THE SAME...

WITH THE SAME WEIRD PLATITUDES...
Bethany Lutheran Church
GOD PREFERS KIND ATHEISTS OVER HATEFUL CHRISTIANS

THE SAME RUMBLING IN MY GUTS, THE SAME WOBBLE IN MY KNEES...
GRUMBLE

THE SAME MUSTY SMELL OF CHURCH BASEMENTS...

AND THE COFFEE—

YUCK! DON'T EVEN GET ME STARTED ON THE COFFEE.
P'TEW!

Abstinence
THE SAME 12-STEP LITERATURE LINED ALL THE TABLES...

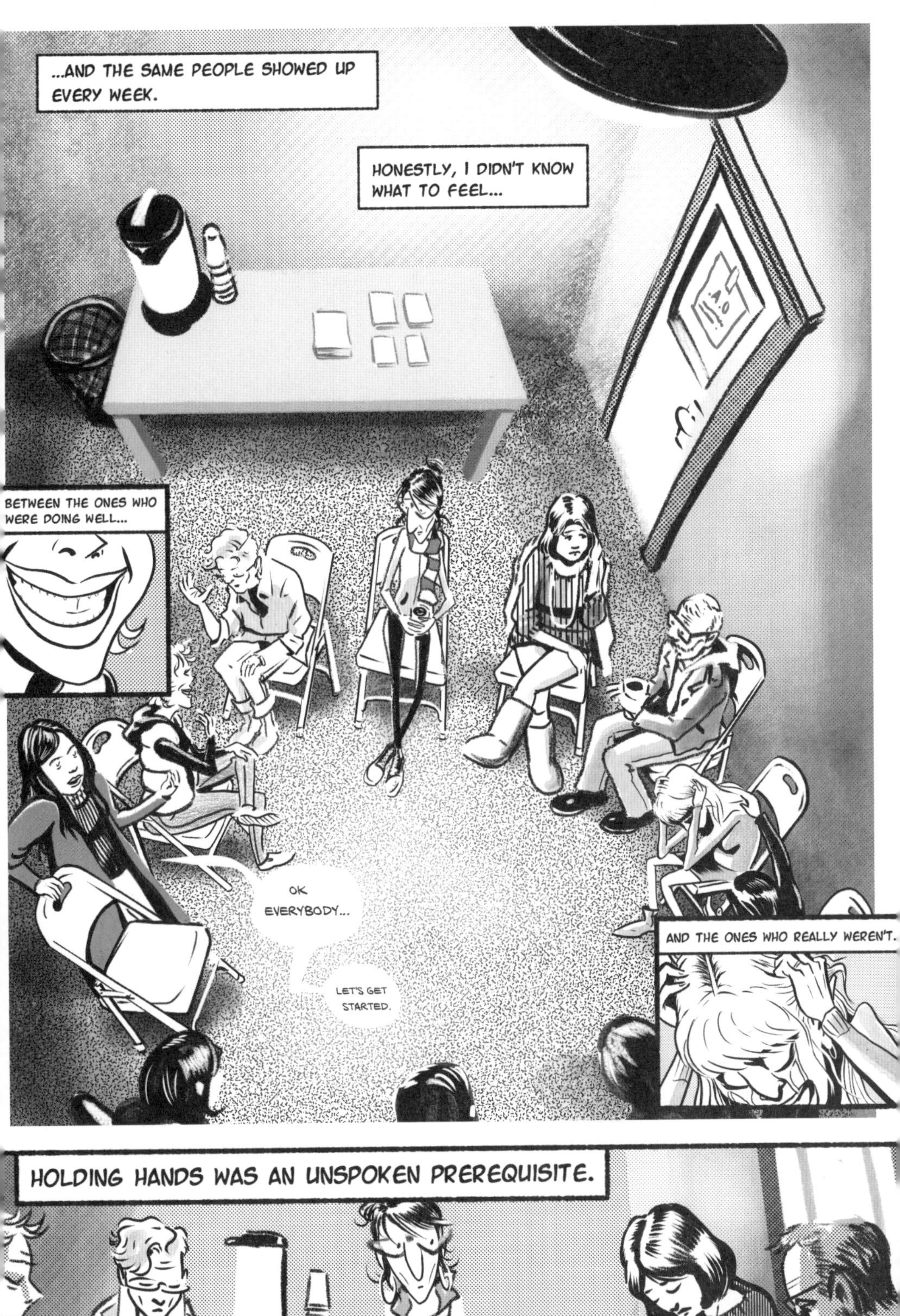
...AND THE SAME PEOPLE SHOWED UP EVERY WEEK.
HONESTLY, I DIDN'T KNOW WHAT TO FEEL...
BETWEEN THE ONES WHO WERE DOING WELL...
OK EVERYBODY...
LET'S GET STARTED.
AND THE ONES WHO REALLY WEREN'T.

HOLDING HANDS WAS AN UNSPOKEN PREREQUISITE.

GOD...
GRANT ME THE SERENITY TO
THE COURAGE TO CHANG

ACCEPT THE THINGS I CANNOT CHANGE...
THE THINGS I CAN...
AND THE WISDOM TO KNOW THE DIFFERENCE...

EVEN SAYING THE WORD "GOD" MADE MY SKIN CRAWL...
SO DOES ANYBODY HAVE SOMETHING THEY'D LIKE TO SHARE ?
I'LL START.
BUT EVEN IF I DIDN'T BELIEVE IN GOD, I DID BELIEVE IN ONE THING FOR SURE...

...I BELIEVED THAT MY LIFE WAS FUCKED.

SO I SHOWED UP WHERE PEOPLE TOLD ME I COULD FIND THE FIX...

...TO SPEND LONG, HOPELESS EVENINGS WITH MY HEAD BURIED IN MY HANDS.

IT WAS REALLY, REALLY HARD... BUT LAST NIGHT I... I ATE ICE CREAM WITH MY GIRLFRIEND.
I WAS SO SCARED...
...BUT I DID IT!
TO BE AROUND PEOPLE WHO HAD A CLUE ABOUT WHAT I WAS GOING THROUGH...

TO BREATHE.

WITHOUT
CHOKING.

ON
CALORIE
CALCULATIONS.

to
RECOVER

...WHATEVER THAT MEANT.

THANK YOU, BROOKE.
WOULD ANYONE ELSE LIKE TO SHARE?

ANYONE?
OK, I'LL GIVE...

Chapter 1

YOU SEE...
...I WASN'T ALWAYS SICK.

I GREW UP PUNK. SO PART OF ME WAS USED TO GETTING EMOTIONAL IN A BASEMENT.
JONESTOWN!
AINT GOT

NOTHIN' ON US!!!
IT JUST USED TO BE A WHOLE LOT LOUDER.

THE PUNK SCENE TAUGHT ME A LOT...
NOT THE LEAST OF WHICH WAS THAT SOCIETY'S BEAUTY STANDARDS WERE SHIT!

NICE LEGS, DYKE!
AND TO TRULY, DEEPLY NOT GIVE A FUCK WHAT THE NORMS THOUGHT.

TO BE REAL, THE ONLY VALUABLE THING I LEARNED IN HIGH SCHOOL WAS THAT I WAS NEVER GONNA BE "NORMAL."
UGH!

THINGS LIKE SPORTS, PROMS, FANCY CARS, AND FASHION DIDN'T INTEREST ME.
WHEREHOUSE
WISH I DIDN'T HAVE TO BRAVE THE NORM-STORM...

...JUST TO GET THE GOODS!
TEAM DRESCH
Personal Best
I HAD A MILLION BETTER THINGS TO FOCUS ON.
I WAS BUSY!
MAKING MIXTAPES
WRITING MANIFESTOS
TAP TAP TIP TAP
READING ALL THE BOOKS
RIDING MY BIKE
TRIBL
SEPT 25 GILM
ALL AGES
GOING TO SHOWS
TAKING POLAROIDS
Attica
STAPLING COPIES OF MY ZINE
AND, OF COURSE, DRINKING AS MUCH COFFEE AS I COULD!

BUT EVEN WITH ALL OF MY POSITIVE RADICAL AND FEMINIST INFLUENCES...
KATHLEEN HANNA
ASSATA SHAKUR
SANDRA CISNEROS
SOMEWHERE WAY IN THE BACK OF MY MIND THE SEED OF AN IDEA WAS WAITING TO SPREAD.

NO MATTER HOW FAR AWAY FROM A "NORMAL" GIRL I WAS.
...NO MATTER HOW MUCH
FEMINIST
LITERATURE
I DEVOURED..
NO MATTER HOW MANY
BIKINI KILL
RECORDS
I OWNED...
DEEP INSIDE,
I THOUGHT I WAS MAYBE
JUST
A
LITTLE
TOO BIG

BUT NONE OF THOSE DEEP DOWN FEELINGS OF BIGNESS EVER HELD ME BACK FROM *GETTING BUSY.*

BY THE TIME I WAS TWENTY-ONE I HAD DATED A HANDFUL OF BOTH *DUDES* AND *LADIES...*
IT WAS EASIER TO NOT WASTE TIME STRESSING OUT ABOUT MY BOD WHEN I COULD GO ON COOL DATES INSTEAD.

MY EARLY LOVE LIFE WAS EXCITING AND ADVENTUROUS, AND MOST OF THE FOLKS I DATED WERE COOL CREATIVE PEOPLE.

THERE WAS JORDAN, THE PUNK SINGER WHO I SANG ALONG WITH AT EVERY BASEMENT SHOW.

MACEY, THE DJ WHO KEPT ME DANCING TIL 4AM.

AND HENRY, THE ARTEEST, WHOSE WORK ETHIC CAPTIVATED AND ENTRANCED ME.

BACK THEN...
I BASED A LOT OF MY SELF-ESTEEM ON THE PEOPLE I DATED.

HONESTLY, IT SUCKS TO ADMIT THIS...

...BUT I NEVER FELT BETTER ABOUT MYSELF THAN WHEN I WAS THE OBJECT OF SOME BABE'S AFFECTIONS

BABES LIKE
HENRY...

DATING **HENRY** WAS A REALLY
FORMATIVE EXPERIENCE
IN MY LIFE...

...AND I CAN'T *TRULY*
BEGIN TO TELL YOU
ABOUT HOW
I GOT
SICK...

...OR
ABOUT MY
RECOVERY...

...WITHOUT TALKING
ABOUT HIM **FIRST**

YOU MIGHT BE ASKING YOURSELF, "*WHAT'S SO GREAT ABOUT THIS GUY?*"

HENRY HAD A TON OF GREAT QUALITIES.

HE WAS GENEROUS.
LET ME GET YOUR COFFEE TODAY.
HE WAS INQUISITIVE.
NO, SERIOUSLY...
letigre
WHAT IS YOUR TAKE ON CASSAVETES ?
HE WAS AMBITIOUS.
YOU INSPIRE ME...
...I WANT TO PAINT A LIFE-SIZE PORTRAIT OF YOU...
OK...
IT'S LIKE THIS PERSON JUST APPEARED WITH THE POWER TO MAKE ME FEEL PRETTIER AND MORE SPECIAL THAN ANYONE EVER HAD BEFORE.

HENRY HAD BEEN MY DOWNSTAIRS NEIGHBOR IN THIS TOTALLY SHITHOLE APARTMENT COMPLEX IN NORTHEAST PORTLAND...
EASTWOOD
I HAD ALWAYS THOUGHT HE WAS A TOTAL CUTIE.

HEY, HI, HELLO...
OVER HERE, DUMMY!
BUT NO MATTER HOW HARD I TRIED TO CATCH HIS EYE...

...HE NEVER SEEMED TO NOTICE ME.
...
AND THEN HE MOVED AWAY.

A WHOLE YEAR PASSED BEFORE WE FINALLY MET.
BY THAT POINT I WAS WORKING AS A COUNSELOR AT A TRANSITIONAL HOUSING SERVICE FOR HOMELESS YOUTH.

IT WAS A TOTALLY COOL JOB, BUT I WAS IN SCHOOL, TOO, AND I HAD TO WORK A LOT OF *OVERNIGHTS*...

...AND I AM **NOT** A *NIGHT OWL*.

BLOOP
I'M AWAKE!

MOSTLY, I SPENT A LOT OF TIME ON THE INTERWEB...
OH YEAH... THAT GUY!
IT WAS AN EXTRA RAD SURPRISE WHEN **HENRY'S** NAME POPPED UP ON MY SCREEN ONE NIGHT.

Henry:
Hey, back when you lived upstairs how come we never hung out?
Lacy:
...

Henry:
Hey, back when you lived upstairs how come we never hung out?
Lacy:
I don't know, but we should make up for it now...

I DIDN'T EVEN KNOW IF I REALLY LIKED HIM YET.
HENRY WAS JUST ANOTHER DATE...
PNCA
NBD.
BUT WHEN I CAME OUT OF CLASS AND SAW HIM THERE WAITING FOR ME...
MY HEART STARTED TO RACE.
BUMP
BUMP
BUMP
HENRY.
OH,
THERE YOU ARE...
...I JUST TEXTED YOU.
HI!
AND THEN RIGHT OFF THE BAT...
HE STARTED SPEAKING MY LANGUAGE.
FLIP
SO, CAN I TAKE YOU FOR A CUP OF COFFEE?
OK...
BUMP
BUMP
BUMP
BUMP
BUMP
BUMP

SO...
WHAT KIND OF ART DO YOU MAKE?
WELL...
IT'S SORT OF COMPLICATED.

OH, I CAN HANDLE COMPLICATED.
I *PREFER* COMPLICATED.

SO SPILL IT.

OK, SMARTY-PANTS...
BUT YOU ASKED FOR IT.
I DID. NOW TALK.

WELL,
MOSTLY, I GUESS IT'S ABOUT
DISCOMFORT.
BUT...

IT'S MORE LIKE HOW DISCOMFORT IS FORMATIVE AS AN EMOTION.
LIKE...

LIKE HOW IT RELATES TO EVERYDAY LIFE,
AND MEMORY!
AND...

UH-

AND?
AND WHAT?

SEX...

HA HA HA
HA HA
HEY!
WHAT'S SO FUNNY?

NOTHING, NOTHING... I THINK THAT'S GREAT.
SO...
THOUGHTS, FEELINGS,
AND BONING.

YEAH, PRETTY MUCH.
PAINTING?

OH, NO!
I CAN'T DRAW OR PAINT TO SAVE MY LIFE!
BESIDES...

I THINK AS ARTISTS WE NEED TO GROW PAST TRADITIONAL FORMS. WE NEED NEW GENRES, YA' KNOW?
OH, TOTALLY.

BUT YOU'RE PROBABLY SICK OF HEARING ME BLAB.
WHAT ABOUT YOU?
WHAT KIND OF ART DO YOU MAKE?

OK, I FLUBBED IT PRETTY BAD THERE, RIGHT?
I PAINT.
OPEN MOUTH, INSERT FOOT.
C-COOL...
ONLY, IT DIDN'T MATTER THAT MY BRAIN KLUTZED.
HE WASN'T OFFENDED OR DEFENSIVE.
EH, I DON'T KNOW... IT'S PRETTY TRADITIONAL.
RIGHT AWAY, HENRY CAUGHT ON TO MY CLUMSINESS AND SENSE OF HUMOR...
BUT I'M NOT THAT SMART.
I'M PROBABLY BETTER OFF PLAYING IT SAFE WITH THE OLD GENRES.
...AND, MORE IMPORTANTLY, HE COULD PLAY ALONG.

WE DIDN'T KISS ON THE FIRST DATE...

NO MAKE-OUTS ON THE SECOND DATE EITHER...

ORRRRRR THE THIRD.

PRETTY SOON WE WERE TAKING NAPS TOGETHER AT MY APARTMENT.
STILL NO KISSES, THOUGH.

AND I COULDN'T HELP BUT WONDER...

WAS IT *ME?*
AND IF SO, WHAT MADE ME SO UNKISSABLE?
I HAD SOME THEORIES...

I WANTED TO BELIEVE IT WAS SOMETHING SIMPLE.
BAD BREATH I COULD JUST BRUSH AWAY...
OR A STAINED OUTFIT I COULD SIMPLY CHANGE OUT OF.

BUT WHAT I REALLY FELT WERE THOSE FEELINGS OF BEING "JUST A LITTLE TOO BIG."
AND THOSE FEELINGS...
THOSE DIDN'T GO AWAY.
HENRY?
YOU OK?

YEAH.
I BROUGHT YOU A PRESENT...

UM,
THANKS?
WHAT IS IT?

IS IT ALIVE?
HA. KIND OF.
I NOTICED YOUR NEIGHBORHOOD HAS A TON OF PLUM TREES, SO I PICKED YOU SOME ON MY WAY OVER.

YOU FORAGED FOR ME?
I GUESS.
WOW!

LACY.
HEY...
WE NEED TO TALK.

OH MY GOD, I THOUGHT...
I'M EATING A BREAKUP PLUM.

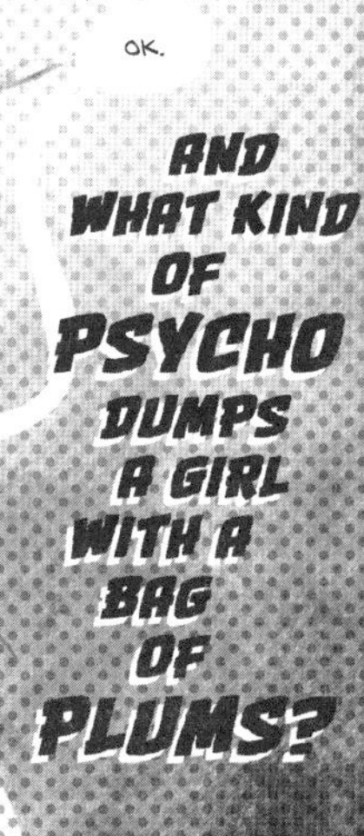
I'M GROSS AND UGLY AND DRIPPING WITH FRUIT JUICE
AND, DUH! OF COURSE HE OULDN'T WANT TO MAKE OUT WITH ME...
GULP
OH...
OK.
AND WHAT KIND OF PSYCHO DUMPS A GIRL WITH A BAG OF PLUMS?

BUT I WASN'T GETTING DUMPED...

SO...
I USED TO HAVE A HEROIN PROBLEM.

HENRY HAD FINALLY DECIDED TO LET ME IN.

IS IT *WRONG* TO ADMIT
THAT THE THING I FELT
MOST IN THAT MOMENT
WAS
RELIEF?

YEAH...

PROBABLY.

Chapter 2

HENRY AND I WERE
A
COUPLE.

LIKE...
POWELL'S
USED & NEW
...A REAL COUPLE.

COMPLETE WITH SMOOCHING...
AND, WELL... YOU KNOW...

HEY...
DID YOU WANT TO...
YES!
I MEAN...
OK.
FINALLY!

I WAS TWENTY-TWO YEARS OLD AND SUPER IN LOVE.
AND AS FOR HENRY'S BIG **REVEAL**...

I CHOSE TO IGNORE IT.
I MEAN, HIS STORY WAS PRETTY GNAR...

SO...
...I USED TO HAVE A HEROIN PROBLEM.

WELL...
ACTUALLY MORE OF AN EVERYTHING PROBLEM.

HEROIN WAS THE WORST, THOUGH.

BUT EVEN WHEN I SHOULD HAVE BEEN REPULSED...
MINOR THREAT

BEFORE THAT IT WAS *SPEEDBALLS.*
HEROIN WAS IN THERE TOO, BUT I SNORTED IT...
SO IT KIND OF DIDN'T COUNT.
I CHOSE TO SEE HIM AS *BRAVE.*

METH WAS A PROBLEM TOO, AT ONE POINT.

I PROBABLY WOULDN'T HAVE STARTED INJECTING...BUT ONE DAY I WAS SMOKING A CIGARETTE WHILE I WAS SNORTING...

...IT COLLAPSED MY LUNG.

I HAD TO STOP SNORTING SHIT...
AND I COULDN'T SMOKE ANYMORE WITHOUT IT BURNING...

SO I WENT FOR THE NEEDLE.
OH...
HENRY.

YEAH.
BUT LISTEN...

...I'M SOBER NOW.
AND I WANTED YOU TO KNOW ALL OF THIS BEFORE—
WELL, YOU KNOW— BEFORE ANYTHING **HAPPENED** BETWEEN US...

HERE WAS SOMEONE WILLING TO BE *VULNERABLE*, AND *SENSITIVE* TO THEIR PARTNER'S WELL-BEING. I COULDN'T SAY THAT ABOUT MOST OF THE OTHER FOLKS I HAD DATED...

ONCE HENRY AND I BECAME OFFICIAL...
...IT WAS ONLY NATURAL THAT HE WANTED TO INTRODUCE ME TO HIS FRIENDS.
MOSTLY, THEY WERE PEOPLE HE HAD MET IN RECOVERY.

THERE WAS KIRK...
LIKE, HOW DID THIS SHIT EVEN GET IN?
...THE PHOTOGRAPHER.

JOSH, WHO WAS CONVINCED THAT MARIJUANA WAS HIS GATEWAY DRUG.
I WAS JUST LIKE...
...GONE, YOU KNOW?

AND POPPY, A RECOVERING METH HEAD COVERED IN STICK'N POKE TATTOOS.

THEY WERE ALL NICE, BUT THE WHOLE NIGHT I WAS ON EDGE...WAITING TO MEET THE ONE FRIEND WHO REALLY MATTERED.

HER NAME WAS GIA.
SIX-FOOT-TALL, GREAT-RACK, TALKS-WITH-HER-HANDS, EX-ADDICT GIA.
AKA HENRY'S BEST FRIEND.

...A BEST FRIEND WHO HE HAD SLEPT WITH A FEW TIMES...
SO...WHAT DO YOU THINK?
IT—
IT'S GOOD.
HEY—

ISN'T THAT...

OH YEAH! WE GOT THEM TOGETHER LAST YEAR.
OH.
...AND WHO HE HAD MATCHING TATTOOS WITH...

...AND WHO HE HAD BEEN IN PAINTING A GIANT LIFE-SIZE PORTRAIT OF.
OH NO! WHAT'S WRONG?
HEY!
IT'S OK!!
WHAT WAS WRONG WAS THAT EVEN THE IDEA OF GIA AND HENRY'S INTIMACY WAS INTIMIDATING.

BABE, HEY... CALM DOWN...
IT'S OK...
I GET IT.

I CAN SCRAP THE PAINTING, OK?
I DIDN'T WANT TO BE THE KIND OF GIRLFRIEND WHO WAS THREATENED BY A FRIEND.
WOULD THAT MAKE IT BETTER?
NO.

...EVEN GLAMAZONIAN TATTOO-SHARING SEXY FRIENDS.
NO WAY, DUDE,

THAT'D BE, LIKE, REALLY SILLY.
I'M OKAY.

THE WORLD NEEDS THAT PAINTING.

THE WORLD MIGHT HAVE NEEDED IT...
BUT HONESTLY, I COULD HAVE GONE WITHOUT IT.
OK, CALM DOWN LACE.
HENRY IS **NOT** INTO HER!

IF HE WANTED TO DATE HER, THEY'D BE DATING!
JUST CHILL OUT.

HI!

CAN YOU BELIEVE HOW BIG HENRY MADE MY TITS?
HE'S CRAZY TALENTED!

OH, I'M GIA, BY THE WAY.
YEAH...

I SORT OF HAD THAT FIGURED.
I'M LACY.

DUH!
I ONLY HAD TO LOOK FOR THE CUTEST BUTTON IN THE WHOLE ROOM!
AND JUST LOOK AT YOU!

LIKE, HAVE YOU SEEN SOME OF THE DWEEBS IN HERE?
JESUS.
NICE FEDORA, ASSHOLE.

HEY!
YOU LIKE WAFFLES, RIGHT?
YOU'RE NOT SOME FREAKY WAFFLE-HATING MONSTER?
UH...

I'M VEGAN, SO...
VEGAN'S NOT A PROBLEM.
I WORK AT THE WAFFLE CART ON DIVIZ... COME VISIT. I'LL HOOK YOU UP!

HERE COMES HENRY.
LET ME GO SAY HEY SO I CAN GET OUTTA HERE.

SO GLAD TO FINALLY MEET YOU, DUDE!
SAME HERE.
OK, SO MAYBE GIA WAS INTIMIDATING IRL TOO...

...BUT SHE WAS CHARMING,
BYE.
AND HER REFUSAL TO LET THINGS BE WEIRD BETWEEN US WON ME OVER.

WHOA.
SO THAT FINALLY HAPPENED...
WHAT DID YOU THINK?
I THINK...

"...I THINK WE'RE GETTING WAFFLES."
THERE YA GO!

WAFFLE TIME
MENU
ALL VEGAN.
LOTSA SYRUP.
LOTSA EARTH BALANCE.
IT LOOKS
RAD AS
HELL!
DUDE!
YOU'RE A
WAFFLE WIZARD!

EH, IT'S ALL IN THE GRIDDLE.
I'M GLAD YOU LIKE IT, THOUGH. THE FOOD HERE IS THE ONLY REASON I TOOK THIS SHIT JOB.
DOESN'T SEEM SO BAD.
POWDER SUGAR

WELL, THE PAY IS CRAP, BUT I EAT FOR FREE. SO IT ALL EVENS OUT I GUESS...
IT'S A LIVING.
HEY—

I GET OUT OF HERE IN LIKE FIFTEEN MINUTES.
YOU GOT ANYTHING GOING ON THIS AFTERNOON?
NOT REALLY.

GREAT! WELL THEN, DO YOU WANNA DRIVE INTO WASHINGTON TO GO ON A POLAROID PHOTO ADVENTURE WITH ME?
POLAROID
IT'LL BE FUUUUUUUUUN...

...AND IT WAS FUN.
SHE TOOK ME TO THIS CRAZY FLEABAG MOTEL.
IT WAS SOOOOO SLEAZY...
UNICORN

BUT AGAIN...
SO FUN!
MNNNN.
AND
GIA!

THAT GIRL IS
A TRIP!
SO
FUNNY!
I WAS SO HAPPY TO FINALLY MEET A FRIEND OF HENRY'S WHO I ACTUALLY HIT IT OFF WITH...

BUT I WAS STILL LEFT WITH THAT LINGERING QUESTION—
SO...
...HOW COME YOU GUYS NEVER DATED?

LIKE, I KNOW THAT YOU GUYS HOOKED UP OR WHATEVER...
...BUT NOW THAT I'VE FINALLY MET HER— SHE'S REALLY COOL!
AND WHATTA...

BABE...
WHAT?

I MEAN...
...I GUESS.
SHE'S...

SHE'S JUST A FRIEND.
AND LIKE...
...SHE HAS A GIANT RACK.

SHUDDER
NOT MY THING.

I PREFER SMALLER...
OH.
THIS CONFUSED THE SHIT OUTTA ME.

LIKE...
GIA HAD A GREAT RACK.

I THOUGHT SHE HAD AN AMAZING BOD ALL AROUND,
BUT AN ESPECIALLY STELLAR BOOB SECTION.
IF HENRY DIDN'T THINK GIA WAS HOT... THEN WHAT THE HECK DID HE SEE IN ME?
HENRY'S DISINTEREST PUZZLED ME.
BUT I TUCKED THAT FEELING AWAY.
THINGS WITH HENRY WERE OBVIOUSLY GOING WELL.

WE HAD FUN TOGETHER.
CATCH ME IF YOU CAN!

HEY... WOULD YOU WANT TO COME HOME WITH ME FOR CHRISTMAS THIS YEAR?
WE WERE MAKING PLANS FOR THE FUTURE.

NO PRESSURE.
THAT'S WHAT REALLY MATTERED. ...RIGHT?

AS THE SCHOOL YEAR TICKED ON, I WAS HAPPY TO SEE HOW ENMESHED OUR LIVES BECAME.

WE DROVE TO THE MOUNTAINS FOR A QUIET THANKSGIVING OF SOAKING IN HOT SPRINGS.

AND LATER THAT WINTER I SAW MY FIRST PORTLAND SNOWFALL WITH HIM.

FOR THE FIRST TIME IN MY LIFE, COLD AND GRAY WEATHER DIDN'T MAKE ME FEEL SO SAD.
WOW!
DO YOU LIKE IT? IT'S AN ANTIQUE TEA SET.
I FIGURED YOU COULD TAKE ONE CUP HOME, AND KEEP ONE HERE AT MY PLACE. THAT WAY YOU'LL ALWAYS HAVE A SPECIAL CUP!

WE WERE COZY TOGETHER.
MWWA

WE WERE WELL CAFFEINATED AND WELL FED.
HENRY...
CAN I TELL YOU A SECRET?
UM, SURE...
WE DIDN'T NEED THE SUN TO STAY WARM.

I'M HAPPY.
BUT I CAN TELL YOU THE EXACT MOMENT WHEN HENRY WENT AWAY...

AGAIN?
IT WASN'T MY RELENTLESS VEGAN COOKING...
LACYLACY LACY!!!
JESUS CHRIST! YOU ALMOST KILLED US!
SORRY...
WATCH THE ROAD!!
IT WASN'T BECAUSE I WAS A TERRIBLE DRIVER.

HENRY...
I'M...
I'M JUST NOT READY.
OR BECAUSE I DIDN'T MOVE IN WITH HIM WHEN HE ASKED.
BURP.
IT WAS BECAUSE FOR THE FIRST TIME IN THE YEAR WE HAD BEEN TOGETHER...I SHOWED UP AT HIS PLACE DRUNK.

IT WAS JUST ONE TIME...
BUT THAT ONE TIME WAS ENOUGH.

HEEEEEEEEEEYYY...

HEY BABE, HOW WAS YOUR END-OF-TERM PARTY?
IT WAS GOOOOOOC

HOW WAS TH—
HIC!
INTERNET?
UH...

ARE YOU DRUNK?

YEAH, THEY HAD—
CHAMPAGNE!!!
WATCH OUT!

OH—
SMASHO!!!

SHIT.

THINGS WENT SWIFTLY DOWNHILL FROM THERE.

WITHIN A WEEK, DINNERS GOT QUIET.

THEN SEX GOT AWKWARD.

WHAT?
NOTHING... JUST...

HEY!

UHHHH...

HE BARELY LOOKED AT ME ANYMORE.

COMMUNICATION TOTALLY BROKE DOWN.

BABE?

MMMH?
I THOUGHT...

I THOUGHT MAYBE I COULD COOK DINNER FOR YOU TONIGHT?

NO.

I ACTUALLY THINK I SHOULD GO TO A MEETING TONIGHT.

I HAVE SOME STUFF I SHOULD TALK TO MY SPONSOR ABOUT.

OH...

...MAYBE LATER?

MAYBE.
HENRY...

I'LL CALL YOU.
OK?

OOOOHKAAAAYYY...
SMEK

CLICK
"OKAY"?

BUT THINGS WERE PRETTY FAR FROM OK.

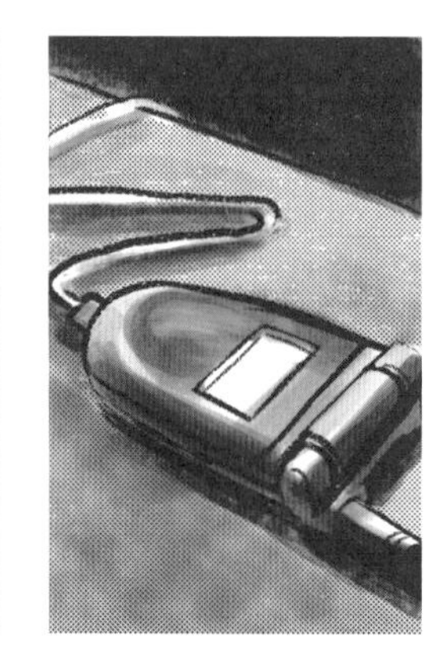

MAYBE YOU'VE BEEN IN A SITUATION LIKE THIS.

BUT ALL YOU CAN DO IS WAIT.

ALL YOU CAN DO...

RITES of SPRING

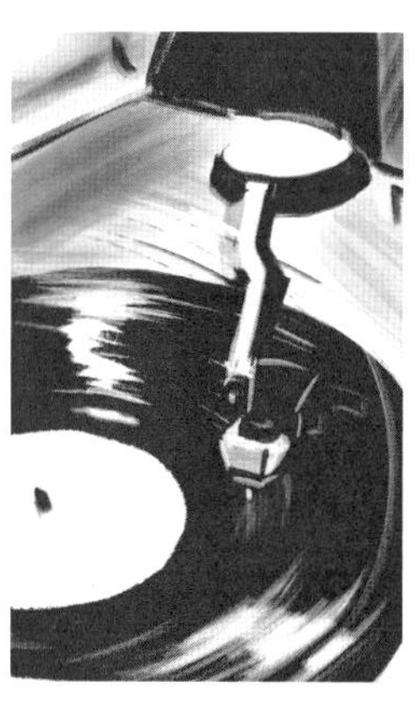

OH, SCREW IT.

RING
RING

HELLO?
DUDE!
WHERE ARE YOU?

YOU KNOW SOMETHING IS WRONG.

IS KILL TIME...

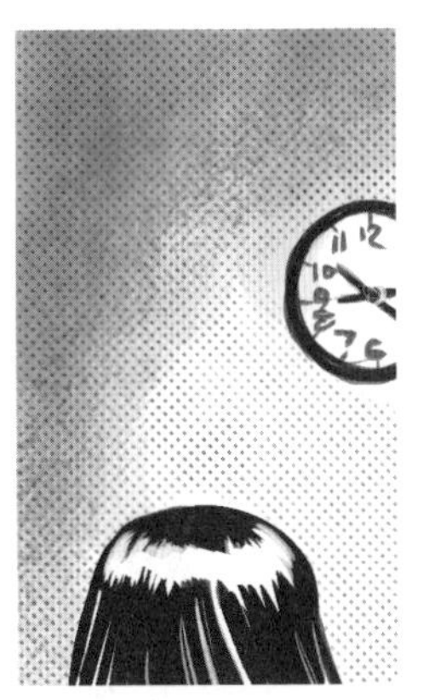

I'M **HOME!**
HENRY! I'VE BEEN WAITING TO HEAR BACK FROM YOU **ALL NIGHT!**

LACY...
LISTEN—

THIS ISN'T WORKING.

THEN HENRY SAID THE ONE THING I ALWAYS ***DREADED*** HEARING...

I'M JUST NOT SURE IF I'M ATTRACTED TO YOU.

OH...

IS IT...
MY BOOBS?
MY BOOBS ARE TOO BIG, RIGHT?
YOU CAN TELL ME.

LACY...NO. JUST— NO! IT'S NOT YOUR BOOBS.
WHAT THEN?
MY THIGHS?
SOME OTHER TOO-BIG PART?

LOOK, I TALKED ABOUT IT WITH MY SPONSOR...
AND IT'S JUST...

LOOK, I JUST CAN'T DO **THIS** ANYMORE.
HENR—

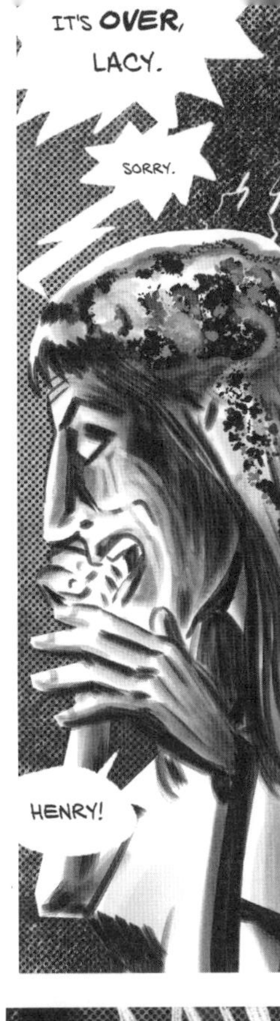
IT'S **OVER**, LACY.
SORRY.
HENRY!

CLICK

AAAHH

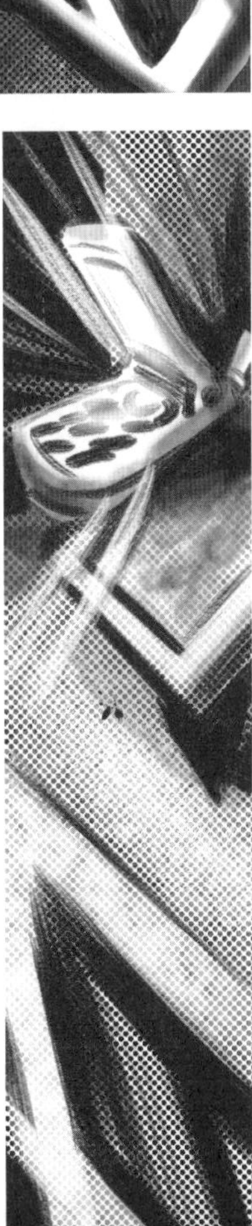

Chapter 3

I
NEVER
CONSCIOUSLY
DECIDED
TO
LOSE
WEIGHT.

I NEVER SAID TO MYSELF...
"HEY, I THINK I'LL JUST STOP EATING."

I STOPPED BECAUSE NO MATTER WHAT I ATE...

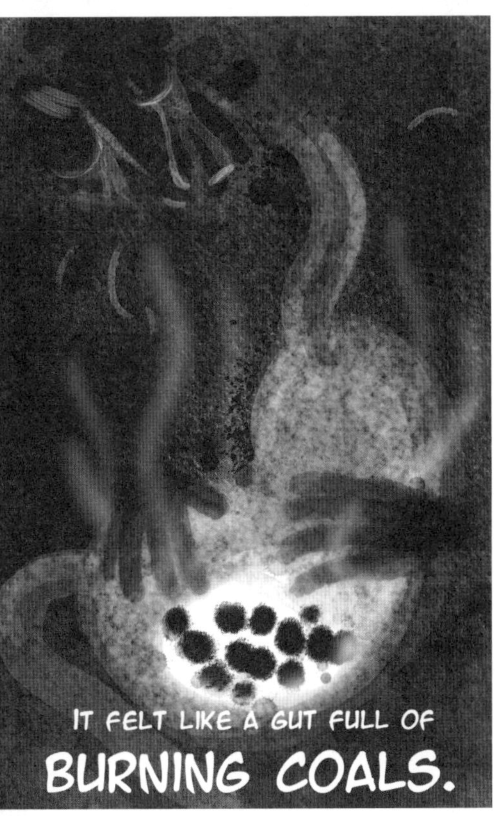
IT FELT LIKE A GUT FULL OF BURNING COALS.

IT WAS BETTER TO JUST BE EMPTY.

I FELT GUTTED ANYWAY...

WHY FIGHT IT?

HELLO?
CLIK!

LACY?
BARK IF YOU CAN HEAR ME...

LACY?
ARF.
BINGO.
DAMN, GIRL.

DUDE!
WHEN WAS THE LAST TIME YOU LEFT YOUR BED?
HRM...

ONE...
TWO...

UH...

FOUR DAYS, I THINK.
6?

HENRY BROKE UP WITH ME.
HE...HE DUMPED ME.

I KNOW, KID.
HE TOLD ME. GAVE ME HIS KEY.
WHAT DO I DO?

IT'S GONNA BE OK.

SNIFF SNIFF
OR IT WILL BE, AFTER YOU SHOWER.
YOU STINK, KID!

YEESH.

?

HEY.

HEY YOU.
GUESS WHAT TIME IT IS?

WHAT?

IT'S TIME TO EAT A FUCKING SANDWICH.

I DUNNO, GIA...
EVER SINCE... I DUNNO. I JUST LOST MY APPETITE. NONE OF THIS LOOKS GOOD TO ME.
OOH!

SPARKLING WATER
WATER?

SERIOUSLY? **SERIOUSLY??**
DUDE!
WE CAN DO BETTER...

...MUCH BETTER!

HA!
I DON'T KNOW, G...

WATER ISN'T FOOD.

EAT UP.

C'MON, KID!
BEST VEGAN SCOOPS IN TOWN!

I'M JUST NOT SURE IF I'M ATTRACTED TO YOU.

I...
I CAN'T.
I'M SORRY!

HEY, HEY!
IT'S OK!

WE'LL TRY AGAIN TOMORROW.

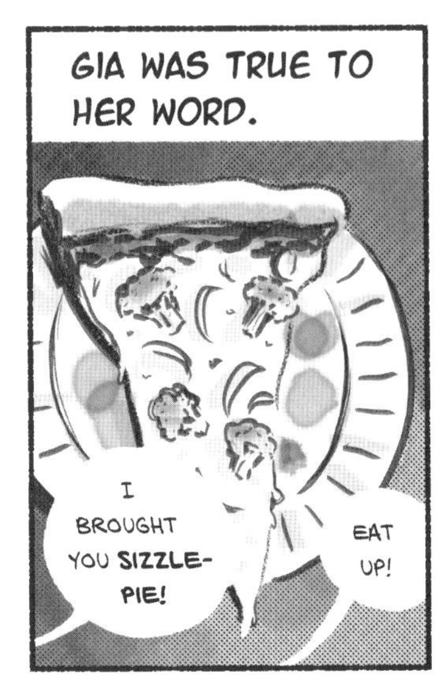
GIA WAS TRUE TO HER WORD.
I BROUGHT YOU SIZZLE-PIE!
EAT UP!

HEY DAVIS, DRINK YOUR SMART-JUICE!
SHE SHOWED UP FOR ME EVERY DAY. SHE FED ME...

AND MADE SURE I GOT SOME MUCH-NEEDED REST.
SERIOUSLY, TAKE 'EM.
AT THIS POINT WE JUST NEED TO KNOCK YOUR ASS OUT.

UH.
THAT'S VERY DRUG ADDICT OF YOU.

THAT'S WHY YOU'RE TAKING THEM, NOT ME.

GIRL, WHEN WAS THE LAST TIME YOU SLEPT?
I GUESS?

THAT'S WHAT I'M TALKIN' ABOUT.
ZZZZZZ

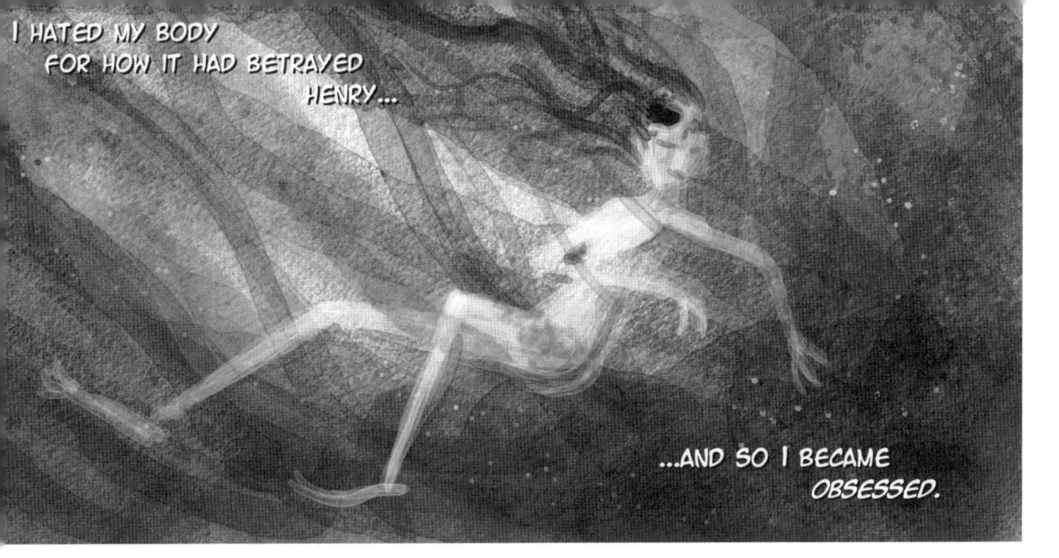
I HATED MY BODY FOR HOW IT HAD BETRAYED HENRY...
...AND SO I BECAME *OBSESSED.*

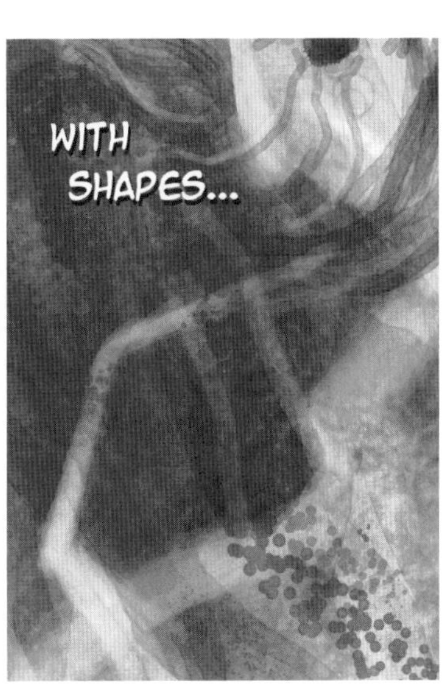
WITH SHAPES...

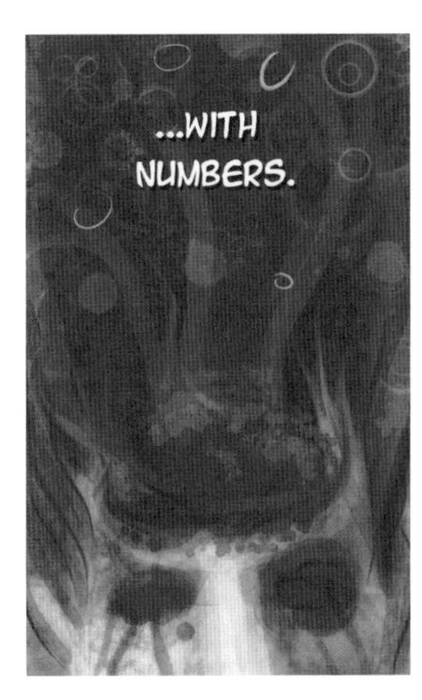
...WITH NUMBERS.

WITH TRYING TO NOT FEEL LIKE HUMAN GARBAGE.

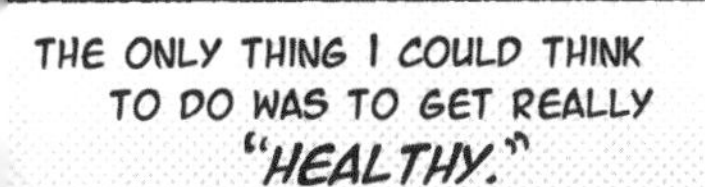
THE ONLY THING I COULD THINK TO DO WAS TO GET REALLY *"HEALTHY."*

Aunt Jen's
OMG! ARSENIC!

I'D NEVER THOUGHT ABOUT HEALTH BEFORE, AND SUDDENLY IT SEEMED LIKE I'D BEEN DOING EVERYTHING WRONG.
FAT CAUSES HEART DISEASE!

MOST FOODS I ENJOYED WERE *HIGHLY TOXIC* ***POISON!***
PHYTIC ACID!!!

IF GIA WAS GOING TO *INSIST* THAT I EAT, IT HAD TO BE FOOD THAT WAS *CLEAN.*
AND EVEN THEN...

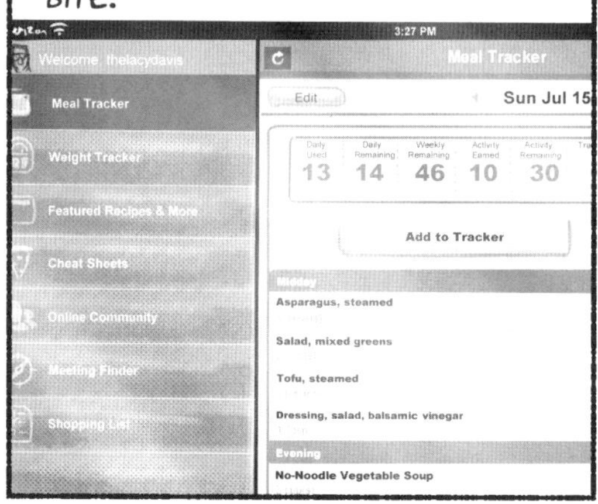
EVERYTHING WAS RECORDED, LIKE, *METICULOUSLY.* DOWN TO THE LAST BITE.
3:27 PM
Welcome, thelacydavis
Meal Tracker
Weight Tracker
Featured Recipes & More
Cheat Sheets
Online Community
Meeting Finder
Shopping List
Meal Tracker
Edit
Sun Jul 15
13
14
46
10
30
Add to Tracker
Asparagus, steamed
Salad, mixed greens
Tofu, steamed
Dressing, salad, balsamic vinegar
Evening
No-Noodle Vegetable Soup

EVERY MOUTHFUL OF FOOD BECAME PART OF AN INTRICATE MATH EQUATION.
SO MANY CALORIES TODAY...
HOW MANY MILES IS THAT?

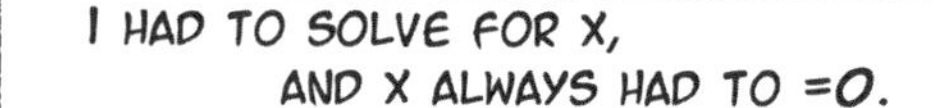
I HAD TO SOLVE FOR X, AND X ALWAYS HAD TO =O.

ALMOST THERE.
KEEP GOING.
EVERY CALORIE WAS ACCOUNTED FOR...

AND THEN SOME—
OK...

ONE MORE MILE.
JUST IN CASE.
AS IF A BODY WERE SOMETHING THAT COULD BE SOLVED.

I WAS TRANSFIXED.
OK, EVERYONE.

OUTSIDE OF RIDING MY BIKE FOR LEISURE, I HAD NEVER BEEN INTO WORKING OUT.
THREE...
TWO...
ONE...
BUT NOW...

NOW, I LOST MYSELF IN THIS NEW FOCUS.
NOW REACH...
AND HOLD.

HUFF
HUH.
HUFF.
I WORKED OUT EVERY CHANCE I GOT.

EVEN WHEN I WAS ON THE CLOCK.
HUH.
HUH.
HUH.
I GOT IN THE HABIT OF SNEAKING TO THE COMPANY GYM DURING MY NIGHT SHIFTS...

...WHEN I WAS *SUPPOSED* TO BE AT MY DESK.
TWO MORE MILES...
YOU HAVE TO.

I WANTED TO LEVEL THE WHOLE THING FOR NOT BEING THE WAY HENRY WANTED.

THE LACK OF ATTRACTION WAS DUE TO MY SHAPE, SO MY *SHAPE* WAS WHAT I WORKED TO CHANGE.

I STILL CRIED MYSELF TO SLEEP EVERY NIGHT...

...BUT AS LONG AS I FELT *HUNGRY*...

I HAD HOPE.

AFTER MONTHS OF MOVING BETWEEN THE GYM AND MY BED, I FINALLY DECIDED TO TRY DATING AGAIN. I NEEDED *SOMETHING* TO DISTRACT MYSELF.
IT WAS WEIRD AT FIRST, HOLDING NEW HANDS...

KISSING NEW LIPS...

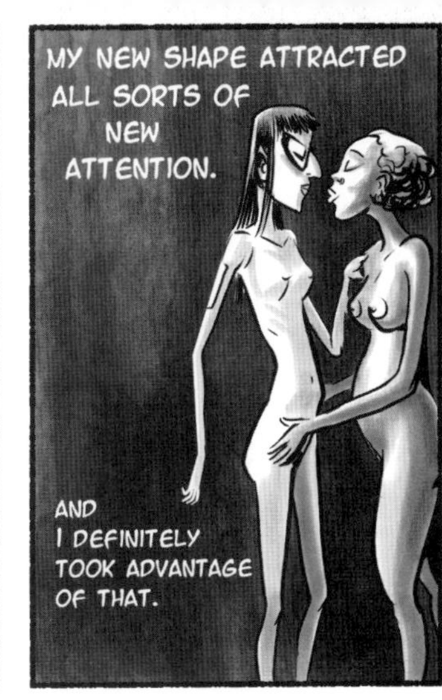
MY NEW SHAPE ATTRACTED ALL SORTS OF NEW ATTENTION.
AND I DEFINITELY TOOK ADVANTAGE OF THAT.

SHE NEVER SEEMED TO NOTICE ME WHEN I WAS BIGGER.
BUT SOMETIMES IT BUGGED ME.

LIKE, PART OF ME WAS DISGUSTED THAT PEOPLE WANTED TO SLEEP WITH ME WHEN I LOOKED LIKE A SKELETON.
WHAT'S WRONG?
NOTHING.
I'M JUST NOT IN THE MOOD.

STILL, IT WAS EASY TO IGNORE THE FACT THAT MY HABITS WERE PROBLEMS WHEN (ALMOST) EVERYONE ELSE DID TOO.
TAP TAP TAP
Lacy: Can't hang tonite...
Gia: Again???
Lacy:Sorry!

YOU MAY THINK MY OBSESSION WITH NUMBERS MEANT I WAS WEIGHING MYSELF ALL THE TIME...
LACY DAVIS?
HERE.
THE DOCTOR IS READY FOR YOU NOW.

...ACTUALLY, I DIDN'T EVEN *OWN* A SCALE.
E
F P
T O Z
L A R S

HI LACY.
I'M DR. O'HARE.

ANY REASON FOR YOUR VISIT TODAY?
NO...JUST A NORMAL CHECKUP.

OK. WELL LET'S START WITH THE BASICS.

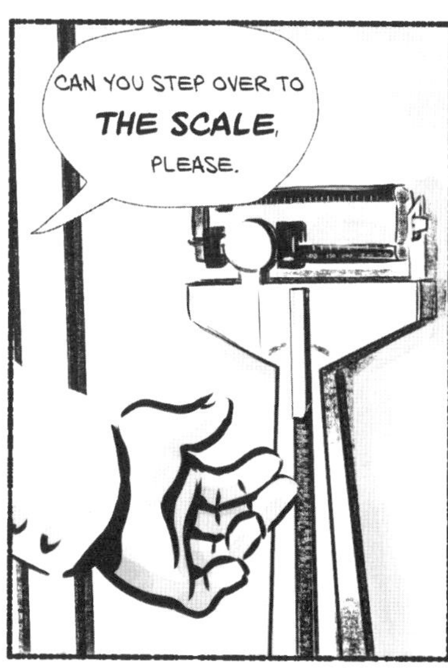
CAN YOU STEP OVER TO **THE SCALE**, PLEASE.

OH.
OK.

STAND TALL.
OK. NOW TURN AROUND, PLEASE?

HMMMMNNN.

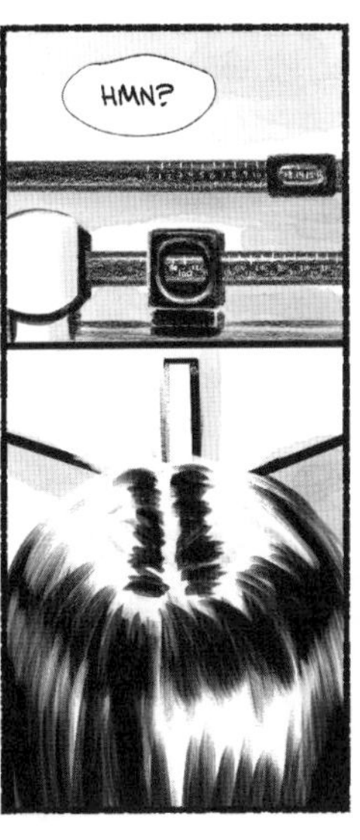
HMN?

I HAD BEEN OBSESSING ABOUT GETTING *SMALLER*...
...BUT NOW "SMALLER" WAS QUANTIFIABLE.

NOW I HAD A NEW NUMBER FOR MY EQUATION.

IT SEEMS YOU'VE LOST A BIT OF WEIGHT THIS YEAR...

I GUESS...
BY OUR RECORDS YOU'VE DROPPED TWENTY POUNDS.

IS THAT...
BAD?

HMN?
OH.

NOT AT ALL!
YOU LOOK GREAT!
AND NOW THAT I KNEW THAT NUMBER...

I *NEEDED* TO CHECK IT *EVERY DAY.*
0.00

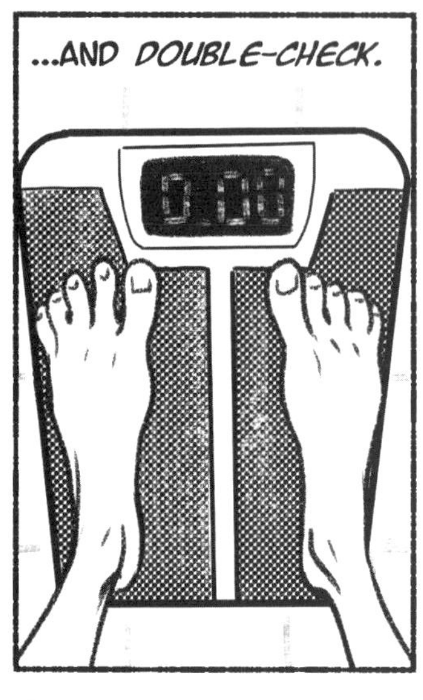
...AND *DOUBLE-CHECK.*

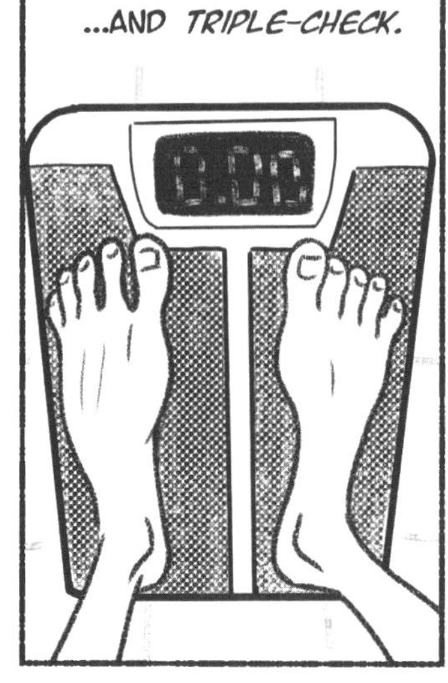
...AND *TRIPLE-CHECK.*

AFTER EVERY MEAL. AFTER EVERY WORKOUT. THE DESIRE TO KNOW WAS A BLOTCH IN MY MIND...

...IMPOSSIBLE TO IGNORE.
HEY LACY.

CAN I HAVE A WORD WITH YOU?
IN MY OFFICE.
I GUESS MY *BEHAVIOR* BECAME IMPOSSIBLE TO IGNORE, *TOO.*

'CAUSE SOON I GOT CALLED OUT AT WORK...
SOME OF *THE CLIENTS* WERE TALKING.
THEY'RE **WORRIED** ABOUT YOU.

AND SO AM I. YOU'VE LOST A **LOT** OF WEIGHT *VERY QUICKLY.*
AND I NOTICED YOU'VE BEEN USING THE GYM DURING YOUR OVERNIGHT SHIFTS.

...AND THEN AT SCHOOL TOO.
FRANKLY, WE'RE CONCERNED.
YOU'VE MISSED MANY CLASSES THIS TERM. YOUR WORK IS SUFFERING.

HAVE YOU BEEN EATING ENOUGH?

SO MY SCHOOL WAS "CONCERNED."
AND MY JOB "ASKED" ME TO TAKE A LEAVE—AS IF I REALLY HAD A CHOICE.

BUT WHO WAS I KIDDING? I COULD BARELY MANAGE MY OWN SHIT...
LET ALONE HELP OUT HOMELESS TEENS.

YOU'D THINK NOT HAVING A JOB WOULD GIVE ME A CHANCE TO REST UP AND GET WELL.
BUT REALLY IT JUST GAVE ME MORE *TIME.*

MOUNTAINS OF TIME.
DRINK **ONLY** WATER—**CHECK!**
CHEW EVERY BITE ONE HUNDRED TIMES—**CHECK!**
ENOUGH TIME TO COMB THE MESSAGE BOARDS OF EVERY WEIGHT LOSS WEBSITE FOR *TIPS AND HACKS.*

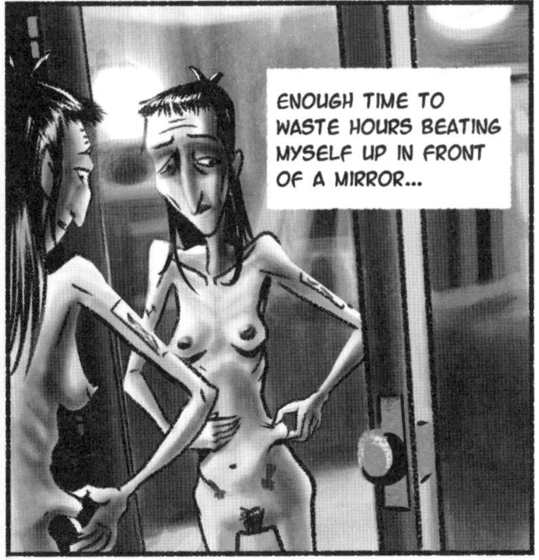
ENOUGH TIME TO WASTE HOURS BEATING MYSELF UP IN FRONT OF A MIRROR...

PINCHING EVERY LOOSE BIT OF FLESH UNTIL IT BRUISED.
AND EVEN **MORE** TIME...

...FOR EXERCISE.
MORE AND MORE EXERCISE.

AND SADLY,
LESS AND LESS
TIME...

...FOR FRIENDS.
WHAT'S LOOKING GOOD, LACE?
UH...
I DON'T KNOW, G...

GIA WAS FINALLY ABLE TO TRACK ME DOWN AND DEMAND SOME FACE TIME.
YOU FOLKS READY?
SHE'S NOT, BUT I'M GOOD TO GO.

I'LL TAKE THE LARGE VEGAN NACHOS...
AND A SOY-VANILLA MILKSHAKE.
I'D BEEN DODGING HER FOR WEEKS.

I GUESS...
...I'LL JUST HAVE A SMALL CAESAR SALAD.
NO CHEESE...
NO CROUTONS.

AND CAN I GET THAT DRESSING ON THE SIDE?
SURE THING.

THOSE ORDERS WILL BE RIGHT UP!

GIA ALWAYS KEPT IT REAL.
SO, YOU KNOW YOU JUST ORDERED A **TEN-DOLLAR** PLATE OF **LETTUCE**, RIGHT?
BUT, LITTLE-KNOWN FACT...

UM...
IT'S CALLED A **SALAD**, DUDE.
WHAT'S YOUR PROBLEM?
...I DON'T ALWAYS LOVE BEING CALLED ON MY SHIT.

TODAY'S SPECIALS

UHH...
...HERE'S YOUR **SHAKE.**

I'LL JUST LEAVE IT HERE.

SLLLIP

SSSSiiP

HEY.
THIS IS A PRETTY RAD SHAKE...
HERE, TRY SOME.

EW!
NO!
THAT SHIT IS DISGUSTING!

LIKE...
...SO UNHEALTHY.

GIRL...

YOU JUST HULKED OUT ON ME FOR OFFERING YOU A DAMN MILKSHAKE!

LOOK AT YOURSELF.
YOU'RE TREMBLING.
I JUST DIDN'T WANT YOUR FUCKING MILKSHAKE, OK?

LOOK...
I KNOW I'M NO BASTION OF WELLNESS.
I'M A FUCKING **DRUG ADDICT**!

OR A FORMER ONE, ANYWAY...
KNOCK KNOCK
...KNOCK ON WOOD.

BUT LISTEN...
MAYBE IT'S BECAUSE I'M AN ADDICT MYSELF...
BUT I KNOW OBSESSION WHEN I SEE IT.

UM.
HERE'S YOUR ORDER.
ENJOY.

AND **THAT** RIGHT THERE...

...THAT'S **OBSESSION.**

MAYBE IT WAS BECAUSE A REAL FRIEND WAS FINALLY SEEING MY PROBLEM...
...BUT SOMETHING CLICKED.

I KNOW.

I KNOW I'VE BEEN ACTING FUCKING TERRIBLE.
I DON'T **KNOW** WHY.

GOD, I'M SO FUCKING SORRY.
DUDE!
IT'S **OK!**
WE CAN GET YOU HELP!

THERE'S MEETINGS FOR THIS, KID.
LIKE THE ONES I GO TO...

BUT FOR **FOOD.**
IT'S CALLED **OVEREATERS ANONYMOUS.**

BUT I DON'T OVEREAT!
HOLD ON.
I'M GONNA GIVE YOU MY FRIEND SASKIA'S NUMBER.

SHE'S BULIMIC, JUST LIKE YOU!
RRRIP
I KNOW SHE'LL TAKE YOU TO A MEETING!

BUT I'M NOT BULIMIC!
I'M NOT!
AND I WASN'T...YET.

AT LEAST NOT THE KIND OF BULIMIA I WAS AWARE OF.
EXERCISE BULIMIA, LACE...
IT'S A THING.
AND EITHER WAY...

YOU NEED HELP!

PLEASE, JUST DO ME A FAVOR...
TAKE THE NUMBER.

"CALL HER..."

HELLO, SASKIA?

THIS IS LACY.

GIA'S FRIEND.

Chapter 4

MEETINGS FOR OVEREATERS ANONYMOUS OR OA, TOOK PLACE IN A CLUBHOUSE IN NORTHWEST PORTLAND CALLED THE ALANO.

WELL...
HERE WE ARE.

ARE YOU READY?
I GUESS SO?
TRUST ME, LACY...

IT'LL BE OK.

I MEAN, EARLY ON THERE WAS A DECENT CHANCE THAT I WOULDN'T COME BACK.

NOT A TOUCHER, EH?
DON'T WORRY.
IT'S ONLY FOR A SECOND.

WHAT WITH THE HAND-HOLDING...

...AND THE RELIGIOUS OVERTONES...

GOD...GRANT ME THE SERE

I WAS REASONABLY CERTAIN

THAT THIS WASN'T THE PLACE FOR ME.

BUT WHILE I WASN'T THRILLED WITH MOST OF WHAT I SAW, I ***DID*** LOVE HEARING OTHER PEOPLE'S DIRT.

I'D LIKE TO SHARE TONIGHT.
MY NAME IS **SASKIA**...

THE WHOLE STORYTELLING ASPECT OF **OA** INTRIGUED ME.

I'M A BINGE EATER...
...A PURGER...
...AND A RESTRICTOR.

HI SASKIA.
HI EVERYONE.
WHERE TO BEGIN?

THINGS HAVEN'T BEEN SO GOOD LATELY...
...I'VE BEEN BINGEING ON SUGAR.

I PROMISE MYSELF TO DO BETTER EACH DAY.
I SIP TEA...
AND LISTEN TO MY STOMACH GROWL.
THEN THE SUN GOES DOWN...

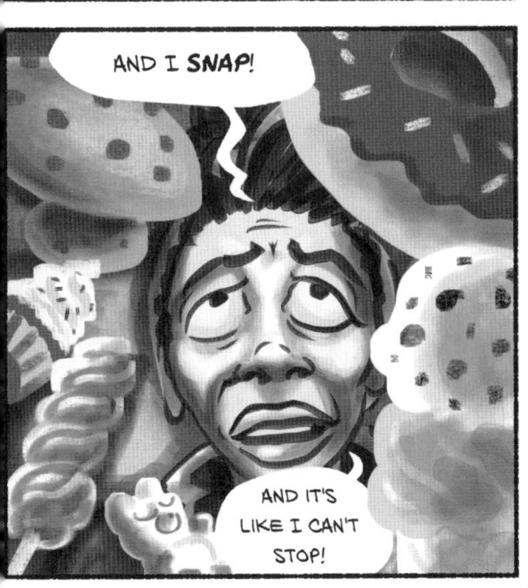
AND I SNAP!
AND IT'S LIKE I CAN'T STOP!

NO MATTER HOW MUCH I FIGHT IT.
BUT...
NO MATTER HOW MUCH THE SCALE KEEPS GOING UP.

...BUT, FOR TODAY AT LEAST...
...I'M **OK** WITH MY NEW CURVES.
AND THAT'S THE **MIRACLE** OF THIS PROGRAM.

I MEAN...I MIGHT NOT WANT TO STAY THIS SIZE FOREVER.
BUT I'M NO LONGER IN A PLACE OF SELF-LOATHING.
NOW I'M JUST WORKING ON MY **PRAYERS** TO HAVE MY URGE TO BINGE REMOVED.

I WAS MOVED BY SASKIA'S STORY. BUT ALL THROUGH THE MEETING, CERTAIN WORDS KEPT STICKING OUT.
AGAIN, NOT MY THING...BUT COULD THESE MEETINGS POSSIBLY BE THE ANSWER TO THOSE *OTHER* SCARY WORDS?
PRAYER
SERENITY
MIRACLE
GOD

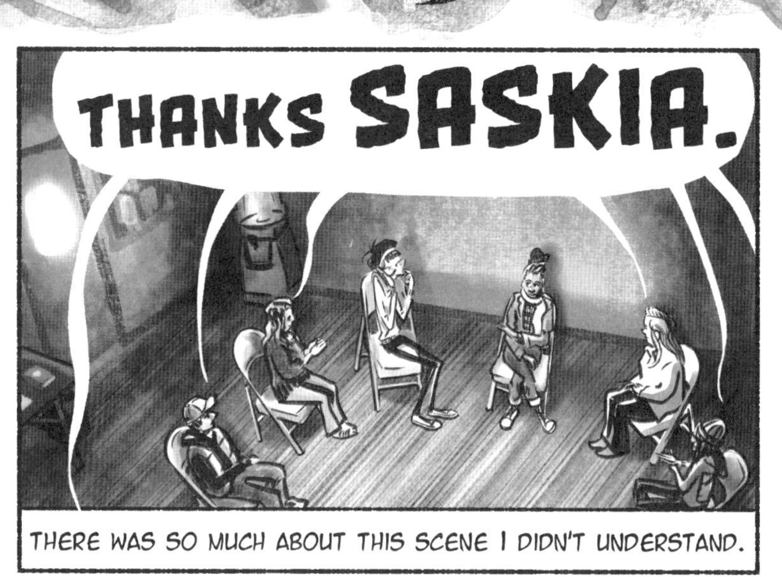
THANKS SASKIA.
THERE WAS SO MUCH ABOUT THIS SCENE I DIDN'T UNDERSTAND.

AT LEAST I KNEW I WASN'T THE ONLY PERSON TRYING TO FIX A SHIT SITUATION WITH FOOD.

I COULD ONLY LISTEN TO SO MUCH DIRT WITHOUT FEELING LIKE I NEEDED TO DISH SOME OF MY OWN.
AT THE END OF MY THIRD MEETING
I DECIDED TO RAISE MY HAND.
HI.

UH...
I'M LACY.
I GUESS...
I GUESS I HAVE A PROBLEM WITH MY DIET.
I THINK IT MAY HAVE GOTTEN OUT OF HAND...
OR SOMETHING.

HI
LACY

AND WHEN I DECIDE TO DO SOMETHING...
HI AGAIN.

...I TEND TO GO ALL IN.
MY NAME IS **LACY.**

HI LACY.
OA LITERATURE SUGGESTS NEWCOMERS ATTEND NINETY MEETINGS IN NINETY DAYS...WHICH I ADMIT IS A LITTLE *CULTISH.*

PREVIOUSLY I HAD SPENT MY TIME COLLECTING LOW-CAL RECIPES, DOING CRUNCHES, AND TRYING TO FIGURE OUT WHAT NORMAL PEOPLE ATE.
YOU SHOULD KEEP COMING BACK.
IT **WORKS.**
I...
I'LL TRY.

EIGHTY-ONE TO GO.
I FIGURED GOING TO MEETINGS WAS AT LEAST A BETTER OPTION THAN ANY OF THOSE.

I'M LACY...
WHERE TO BEGIN?
UM...

I'M COMPLETELY HEARTBROKEN. THE SIGHT OF FOOD DISGUSTS ME. I KNOW THAT I'D STILL BE WITH HENRY IF I HAD A DIFFERENT BODY. BEING SMALL IS THE ONLY THING I HAVE. WHEN I DON'T FEEL HUNGRY, I FEEL VERY VERY AFRAID. THERE ARE SO MANY FOODS AND SO MANY OF THEM ARE SO TOTALLY UNHEALTHY!
BUT I COULDN'T SAY ALL THAT.

SO I SAID WHAT I COULD.
I JUST DON'T...
...I DON'T WANT TO EAT **GARBAGE.**
I MEAN...
I KNOW I SHOULD EAT MORE FOOD IN GENERAL...

...BUT, LIKE, SO MANY FOODS ARE JUST...**JUNK!**
IT'S CONFUSING!

I DON'T EVEN KNOW WHAT TO EAT...
SO...

...SO I DON'T EAT MUCH OF ANYTHING AT ALL.

I'M SORRY.
I...
I THINK I'M DONE.

IN SOME WAYS I WAS GRATEFUL. TWO WEEKS INTO MEETINGS, IT WAS COMFORTING TO KNOW I WASN'T ALONE IN MY THOUGHTS ABOUT FOOD...
AND EVEN MY INITIAL SHARES FELT GOOD.
BUT...
ON THE OTHER HAND, SUGGESTING THAT I WAS POWERLESS REALLY RANKLED ME.
HOW WAS I SUPPOSED TO SPILL MY GUTS AND PLEDGE ALLEGIANCE TO SOME WACK-ASS IDEA OF GOD?
PUNK HAD TAUGHT ME THAT I WAS POWERFUL.
I DIDN'T WANT TO BACKTRACK IN MY THINKING.

HOW WAS TONIGHT'S MEETING?
SIGH
OK, I GUESS...

WELL...

"OK" ISN'T THE WORST...
...IS IT?

I DON'T BELIEVE IN GOD.

SO?
SO WHAT?
SO...
THAT SEEMS LIKE KIND OF A **BIG DEAL** TO *THESE PEOPLE.*

YOU MEAN...
PEOPLE LIKE ME.

SORRY, G.
BUT...
I JUST DON'T GET IT.
IT FREAKS ME OUT TO TALK SO MUCH ABOUT WEAKNESS.
AND I STILL DON'T EVEN KNOW WHAT I HAVE.

LIKE, I ADMIT THIS DIET HAS GONE **TOO FAR**, BUT THAT DOESN'T MEAN I WANT TO GO TO **CHURCH**.
YOU'RE THINKING ABOUT IT ALL WRONG, DUDE.

YOU THINK ***I*** GO TO **CHURCH**??
HELL, NAW!
GOD IS LIKE...

...IT'S LIKE A CATCHALL TERM, SOMETHING WE USE BECAUSE WE'RE SICK AND CAN'T ALWAYS TRUST OURSELVES.
BUT IT'S NOT LIKE YOU NEED TO PRAY TO AN OLD MAN ON A CLOUD.

IT COULD BE...
WELL, LITERALLY *ANYTHING*. THE UNIVERSE... THE COSMOS... THE MIGHTY THOR... A *ROCK*...

...A **LEAF**, EVEN!
WHATEVER FLOATS YOUR BOAT!

MAYBE YOUR "GOD" IS TRUSTING IN THE GROUP.
THAT'S WHAT ALL THE POWERLESSNESS TALK IS ABOUT.

IT'S NOT THAT WE'RE **WEAK**.
IT'S THAT WE KNOW WE CAN'T HANDLE EVERY SINGLE THING ON OUR OWN.

SOMETIMES IT'S OK TO ADMIT YOU NEED HELP!
JUST LIKE IT'S OK...
TO ASK YOUR PAL FOR A *RIDE HOME.*
TRY THINKING OF IT THAT WAY. SOMETIMES YOU JUST NEED A RIDE.
I DO NEED RIDES A LOT...
TELL ME ABOUT IT.
SPEAKING OF—HERE'S YOUR **STOP.**
THANKS FOR THE RIDE, G.

UGH.
FINE.
STEPS.

CHAPTER 5

SPONSORS ARE A LOT LIKE THERAPISTS.

YOU CAN COMPLETELY UNLOAD ALL OF YOUR PROBLEMS ON THEM WITHOUT JUDGEMENT.

THE **DIFFERENCE** IS THAT THEY WILL ALSO TELL YOU ABOUT THEIR LIFE IN RETURN...

...**AND** THEY'RE TOTALLY FREE OF CHARGE.

STEP ONE:
ADMIT THAT YOU ARE POWERLESS OVER FOOD AND THAT YOUR LIFE HAS BECOME UNMANAGEABLE.

BUT...SOMETIMES WE ALL HAVE REALIZATIONS WE DON'T LIKE, RIGHT?
AND... SORRY, LACY...
BUT I'M PRETTY SURE YOU'RE POWERLESS WHETHER YOU WANT TO BE OR NOT.

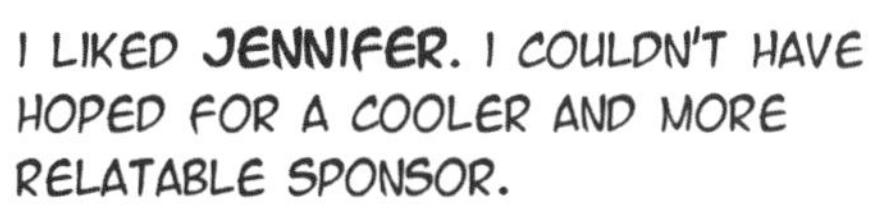
I LIKED JENNIFER. I COULDN'T HAVE HOPED FOR A COOLER AND MORE RELATABLE SPONSOR.

MAYBE...
I GUESS...

AND I CAN SAY THAT! I CAN ASK FOR HELP!
I MEAN, OBVIOUSLY...
OR I WOULDN'T BE SITTING HERE.
BUT POWERLESS?
BUT MOST OF ALL I LIKED THAT I DIDN'T NEED TO HIDE MY THOUGHTS FROM HER.

I THINK THAT LANGUAGE SUCKS!
HMN.
SO, GIA...

SHE'S BEEN A BIG SUPPORT FOR YOU...
ARE YOU KIDDING?
SHE'S THE BEST!
I WOULDN'T BE HERE IF IT WASN'T FOR HER.

DO YOU GUYS HANG OUT OFTEN?
WELL...
SHE CHECKS IN WITH ME REGULARLY, BUT I CAN'T ALWAYS HANG.

HMMN...
WHAT ABOUT OTHER FRIENDS?
OTHER FRIENDS?

WELL, YEAH...
I SEE FRIENDS EVERY DAY...
IN GROUPS.

I KNOW YOU'RE ALWAYS IN GROUP...
...AND THAT'S GREAT.
BUT WHAT ABOUT THE OTHER PEOPLE IN YOUR LIFE, BEFORE ANOREX—

I MEAN—
BEFORE YOUR, UMM...
FOOD PROBLEMS.
AND THERE WAS THE FIRST MENTION OF THE WORD I'D BEEN AVOIDING.

IT'S...IT'S BEEN KIND OF A WHILE, ACTUALLY.
AND WHY IS THAT?

IT'S JUST THAT I GET TIRED, YOU KNOW?
LIKE, SO TIRED.
BETWEEN WORK, SCHOOL...

...AND GOING TO AS MANY MEETINGS AS I CAN... I'M JUST BEAT!
THUD!
AND WHEN FRIENDS DO CALL
THEY ALWAYS WANT TO GET DINNER OR SOMETHING.

YOU'RE CUTTING THE PEOPLE WHO CARE OUT OF YOUR LIFE...
BECAUSE THEY WANT TO EAT WITH YOU?

IS THAT REALLY WORTH IT?
I ALWAYS TRIED NOT TO THINK OF IT...

WHAT I WAS GIVING UP TO MAINTAIN CONTROL.
NO.
WELL THEN, LET ME ASK YOU THIS...

WOULD YOU CONSIDER SHARING A MEAL WITH ME IF I WAS HUNGRY?
EEEEEH...
NO THANKS, JENNIFER.

I CAN'T.
AND I DON'T KNOW WHAT'S IN THE FOOD HERE.

WELL, WHAT ABOUT THIS SOUTHWEST SALAD?
IT SAYS **VEGAN**.

I...
FAT!
PHYTATES!
SALT
CARBS!
...I CAN'T.
BECAUSE YOU'RE SCARED OF WHAT'S IN IT?
LACY...
WHEN YOU LIVE YOUR LIFE MAKING CHOICES BASED ON **FEAR**...
SOME MIGHT SAY YOU'RE...
POWERLESS.

THAT NIGHT AS I PREPARED MY DINNER, I THOUGHT ABOUT EVERYTHING JENNIFER SAID.
AND SASKIA.
AND ALL THE REST.

I LAID OUT A SKIMPY SLAB OF BAKED TOFU, A FEW SLICES OF AVOCADO, AND AS MUCH HUMMUS AS I COULD STOMACH.
IT WAS THE MOST FOOD I COULD IMAGINE EATING IN ONE SITTING.

AND AS I FORCED MYSELF TO EAT THIS MODEST SNACK OF A DINNER...
...I REALIZED...

...I DIDN'T EVEN TASTE FOOD ANYMORE.

I HAD GIVEN ALL OF MY ATTENTION...

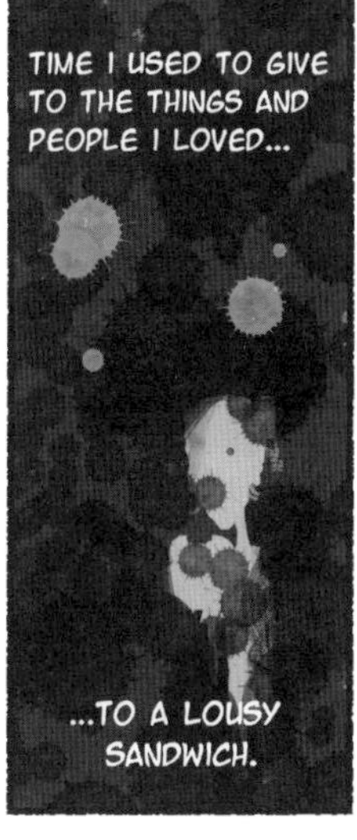
TIME I USED TO GIVE TO THE THINGS AND PEOPLE I LOVED...
...TO A LOUSY SANDWICH.

AND IT TASTED LIKE NOTHING AT ALL.

HI EVERYONE.
I'M LACY...

STEP TWO:
BELIEVE THAT A POWER GREATER THAN OURSELVES CAN RESTORE OUR *SANITY*.

STEP THREE:
MAKE A DECISION TO TURN OUR LIVES OVER TO THE CARE OF *GOD*.
(AS WE UNDERSTAND HIM.)

BY THIS POINT I HAD GIVEN IT A LOT OF THOUGHT.
IT'S HARD.

AND AS WONDERFUL AS GIA'S SUGGESTIONS WERE,
I KNOW IT'S STALE TO STRESS ABOUT GOD HERE.

NONE OF THEM WERE REALLY RIGHT FOR ME.
IT'S JUST, LIKE...
PAR FOR THE COURSE IN OA.

YOU ROCK, ROCK!
BUT DUDES—

HOW AM I SUPPOSED TO TURN MY LIFE OVER TO SOMETHING I DON'T EVEN BELIEVE IN?
AND I MEAN, SERIOUSLY—
HIM?

LIKE, REALLY?
NO OFFENSE,
BUT I CAN'T RECOVER BY THINKING OF SOME—
SOME PATRIARCH IN THE SKY!

I THINK FOR ME, "GOD" HAS TO BE LIKE...
SOMETHING DIFFERENT.

LIKE MY GRANDMOTHER.

GROWING UP, SHE WAS ALWAYS, LIKE, THE MOST IMPORTANT PERSON TO ME.
SHE WAS ALWAYS THERE...

ENCOURAGING ME TO BE SMART.
ARE YOU A BIRD BRAIN...
OR A BIG BRAIN?
BIG BRAIN!
SHE DIDN'T GIVE A DAMN WHAT I LOOKED LIKE.

SHE DIED A FEW YEARS BACK.
BEFORE...
BEFORE I GOT SICK.

WHEN I THINK OF WHAT IT WOULD BE LIKE FOR HER TO SEE ME LIKE THIS...I FEEL SO ASHAMED.
SHE WOULDN'T WANT THIS.

SHE WOULD WANT ME TO DO EVERYTHING I COULD TO GET BETTER.
SO...

MAYBE THAT MEANS BELIEVING IN A HIGHER POWER.
AND IF SO...

...I'M GOING TO BELIEVE IN HER.
BECAUSE I KNOW SHE'D NEVER STOP BELIEVING IN ME.

I ALSO TOOK JENNIFER'S UNSPOKEN ADVICE.
UNICORN
TEL
Inn
42 95 1P WKDY
HB
WEEKLY RATES
VACANCY
I MADE AN EFFORT TO SEE MY FRIENDS.
AND EVEN IF IT WASN'T OVER FOOD...

IT WAS SOMETHING.
SO...

HOW'S 12-STEPPING TREATING YOU?
EH.
IT'S OK.

I'M MAKING SOME PROGRESS.
Flap

FINISHED STEP THREE.
THAT'S **GREAT**!

TELL ME YOU CHOSE THE ***LEAF!***

MY DEAD GRANDMA, ACTUALLY.

AH, WELL. THAT'S PROBABLY FOR THE BEST.
LIFE GETS BETTER AFTER THE THIRD STEP.
FOR REAL?
FOR REAL.

I KNOW SOME OF THE STEPS SOUND CORNY, BUT I DON'T OVERTHINK THE DETAILS.
'CAUSE LEFT TO MY OWN DEVICES I'D BE...
WELL, IN A SHITHOLE LIKE THIS.
ONLY INSTEAD OF TAKING PICTURES, I'D BE SMOKING CRACK, WITH NEEDLES IN BOTH ARMS.

NO JOKE, DUDE.
I GUESS IT DOESN'T ALWAYS SHOW...
BUT I'M A WRECK TOO.

AND I CAN'T EXPLAIN **WHY** GOING TO MEETINGS AND PRAYING KEEPS ME SOBER...
I DIDN'T BEGRUDGE GIA'S METHODS, BUT *SOBER* VERSUS *NOT SOBER* WAS VERY DISTINCT.

MY *WEIRDNESS* AROUND FOOD? NOT SO MUCH.
BUT I'M NOT GONNA COMPLAIN ABOUT IT.

LEAF KNOWS THERE ARE WORSE WAYS I COULD BE SPENDING MY TIME.
MY SICKNESS WAS ALMOST IMPOSSIBLE TO QUALIFY, LET ALONE QUANTIFY.

BUT I WASN'T GOING TO ARGUE WITH GIA'S SOBRIETY.
HEY G.

EVEN IF IT IRKED ME TO THINK I'D NEED TO GO TO MEETINGS FOREVER JUST TO KEEP SANE.
YEAH?

AH!

THANKS!
FOR LETTING YOU BLIND ME?

NAH, DUDE.

I MAY HAVE CHOSEN MY GRANDMA TO BE MY GOD...

BUT I'VE NEVER HAD A FRIEND LIKE YOU!
AH, GEEZ...

WELL DO ME A FAVOR.
KEEP WORKING ON GETTING BETTER.

IF I DON'T SHARE WAFFLES WITH YOU SOON, I CAN'T KEEP TAKING YOU TO SHITTY MOTELS.
NO ONE WANTS THAT.

GIA WAS RIGHT.
THE STEPS DID GET EASIER.

BUT I WOULDN'T SAY I WAS MUCH *HEALTHIER.*
HEY LACY!
HEY.
WOW, YOU'RE LOOKING A LOT BETTER.
I HAD SLOWLY BEGUN TO GAIN BACK A BIT OF WEIGHT AS I WORKED THE FIRST THREE STEPS.

I WAS STILL UNDERWEIGHT, BUT I GUESS I DIDN'T LOOK ***AS MUCH*** LIKE THE TERRIFYING SKELETON I HAD BEEN.
THANKS.
I GUESS I'M JUST DOING WHAT I NEED TO DO.
NOT THAT I WAS REALLY HAPPY ABOUT IT.

EVERY DAY WAS A WEIRD BATTLE OF WILLS.
WELL, I LOOK FORWARD TO SEEING MORE AND MORE SUCCESS!

I WANTED TO KICK THIS EATING DISORDER'S ASS STRAIGHT TO JUPITER...
IF YOU'RE TALKING ABOUT MY **WEIGHT**...
IT'S ACTUALLY JUST **FINE** NOW.

AS LONG AS I DIDN'T ACTUALLY HAVE TO GAIN MORE WEIGHT.
NOT THAT IT'S ANY OF YOUR BUSINESS.
I NEED TO GET TO CLASS.
CLEARLY I HAD A LOT MORE WORK TO DO.

STEP FOUR: MAKE A SEARCHING AND FEARLESS *MORAL INVENTORY* OF OURSELVES.

SURE, WRITING A LIST OF YOUR WORST FLAWS ISN'T THE MOST FUN.

BUT WRITING A LIST IS SURE MORE CONCRETE THAN TRYING TO FIGURE OUT A DEITY.

I WAS A *ZINE KID*.

WRITING WAS SECOND NATURE.

STEP FIVE: ADMIT TO *GOD*, TO *OURSELVES*, AND TO ANOTHER *HUMAN BEING* THE EXACT NATURE OF OUR WRONGS.

SO I KIND OF TACKLED THIS THE ONLY WAY I KNEW HOW...
JENNIFER SAT WITH ME PATIENTLY AS I READ MY NEW ZINE...

...COVER TO COVER.
I CAN'T STOP THINKING THAT I SHOULD BE SMALLER...
every shitty thing.
ADMITTING ALL MY FAULTS TO ANOTHER PERSON DEFINITELY SUCKED!

BUT I WAS SO USED TO BELIEVING I WAS A SHITTY PERSON...
I'M SELF-OBSESSED. I BARELY LISTEN TO OTHERS.
THAT FOR THE MOST PART, IT CAME NATURALLY.

STEP SIX:

ARE ENTIRELY READY TO HAVE *GOD* REMOVE ALL THESE *DEFECTS* OF *CHARACTER.*

HEY GRANDMA...

STEP SEVEN:
HUMBLY ASK ~~HIM~~ HER TO REMOVE OUR SHORTCOMINGS.

MUAH!
THANKS FOR TRYING.

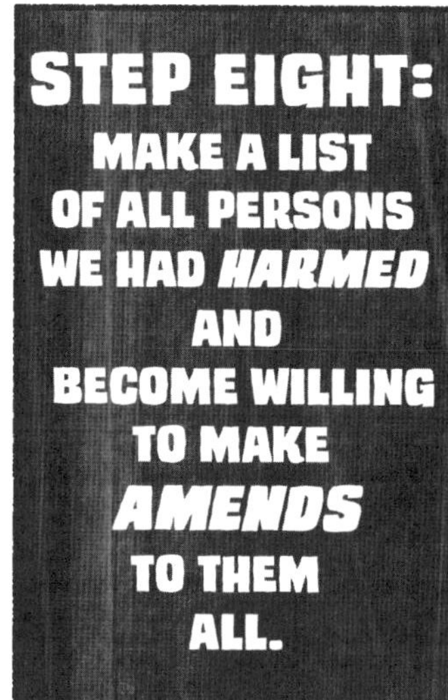

STEP EIGHT:
MAKE A LIST OF ALL PERSONS WE HAD HARMED AND BECOME WILLING TO MAKE AMENDS TO THEM ALL.

ONCE AGAIN, MAKING THE LIST WAS EASY...

STEP NINE:

MAKE
DIRECT AMENDS
TO SUCH PEOPLE WHEREVER POSSIBLE, EXCEPT WHEN TO DO SO WOULD INJURE THEM OR OTHERS.

...MAKING "DIRECT AMENDS"?
12 Luisa
15 Carlos
16 NEW SEASONS

MARKET
IT'S JUST ANOTHER STEP.

UM, EXCUSE ME,
CAN I PLEASE SPEAK TO THE MANAGER?
CUST
SERV
THAT WOULD BE ME.

OK, HERE GOES...
MY NAME IS LACY.
I'M IN A 12-STEP PROGRAM FOR EATING DISORDER RECOVERY.

OK LACE...
NOT SO MUCH.

AND...
I'D LIKE TO MAKE AMENDS.

OOOOOOOOOOH-KAY...
WHAT'S THAT SUPPOSED TO MEAN EXACTLY?

WELL...
...SEE, I'VE STOLEN FROM NEW SEASONS...
...LIKE KIND OF A LOT, ACTUALLY.

I'M SORRY. I KNOW THERE'S NO EXCUSE, BUT...
...A LOT OF MY SICKNESS HAS BEEN ABOUT AVOIDING FOOD.

I USED TO COME HERE SO HUNGRY...

I'D EAT OFF OF THE SHELVES WITHOUT PAYING.
LIKE—
LIKE IF I DIDN'T PAY, IT WAS LIKE IT DIDN'T HAPPEN.

WHICH SIMPLY ISN'T TRUE.
SO I DID SOME MATH...

...AND I FIGURE I OWE YOU $250 FOR STOLEN FOOD.

MAKING AMENDS WASN'T ABOUT SAYING "SORRY."

I COULD SEE ON THIS LADY'S FACE...
HONEY—
SORRY DIDN'T MEAN SHIT.

I DIDN'T NEED TO APOLOGIZE, I HAD TO MAKE THINGS RIGHT.
THERE'S NO WAY TO RING UP THOSE STOLEN ITEMS.
SO I DON'T KNOW WHAT TO TELL YOU EXCEPT...

EVEN IF MY EFFORTS WERE NOT WELL RECEIVED.
...YOU'RE **BANNED** FROM NEW SEASONS.
I'LL BE WATCHING FOR YOU.

I...I GET IT.
SORRY, AGAIN.
HAVE A NICE DAY.

BUT LACY?
Y-YEAH?
I *DO* HOPE YOU GET BETTER.

IT WAS REALLY HARD TO TELL IF ALL MY WORK WITH THE STEPS ACTUALLY MADE ME BETTER...BECAUSE STILL, ALMOST *NOTHING* WAS HARDER FOR ME THAN *PREPARING FOOD.*
MY MEALS WERE STILL STRICTLY CONTROLLED PORTIONS— ALL SECTIONED OFF IN MY LITTLE TUPPERWARES.

AND EVEN WHEN I GOT MY SHIT TOGETHER TO PAY FOR MY OWN FOOD...
...I STILL FOUND IT TOUGH TO SWALLOW.

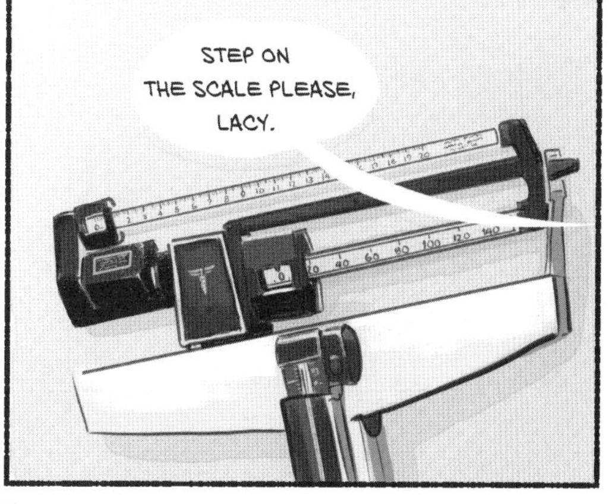
I WANTED TO STAY ACCOUNTABLE TO A PROFESSIONAL, SO I STARTED SEEING MY DOCTOR REGULARLY...
STEP ON THE SCALE PLEASE, LACY.

...A DIFFERENT DOCTOR, OF COURSE.
YOU CAN FACE THIS WAY.
YOU DON'T NEED TO LOOK AT THE NUMBER...
THANKS. NOW STAND TALL.
I FOUND HER BECAUSE SHE ADVERTISED HERSELF AS A FEMINIST PRACTITIONER—
MEANING SHE WASN'T GOING TO PAT ME ON THE BACK FOR STARVING MYSELF.

OK.
I'MAPIGI'MAPIGI'MAPIGI APIGI'MAPIGI'MAPIGI'M APIGI'MAPIGI'MAPIGI'M APIGAPIGI'MAPIGAPIG I'MAPIGPIGPIG—
I SHOULD NEVER HAVE EATEN THAT 'NANNER.

ALL GOOD, LACY.
YOU CAN STEP DOWN.

IN MY EARS "**GOOD**" STILL TRANSLATED TO "***BIG.***"

MOVES, YES...
BUT THE THINGS I USED TO DO...
FOR A BALLERINA BODY?

WELL, THEY WEREN'T GREAT.
AT A CERTAIN POINT I HAD TO CHOOSE...
THE BALLET?

OR ME?
I CHOSE ME.
AND I THINK YOU CAN TOO—

BUT YOU NEED TO BE WILLING TO GAIN WEIGHT.
YOU NEED TO ACCEPT THAT YOUR BODY WILL CHANGE.

CAN YOU DO THAT?
IF I'M HERE TO HELP YOU?
NONONONONO NONONONO NONONONO NONONO...
NO WAY.
OA HAD GIVEN ME A LIST OF TASKS TO CHECK OFF—

BUT ACCEPTING MY BODY?
I MEAN...
YES.
I'LL TRY.

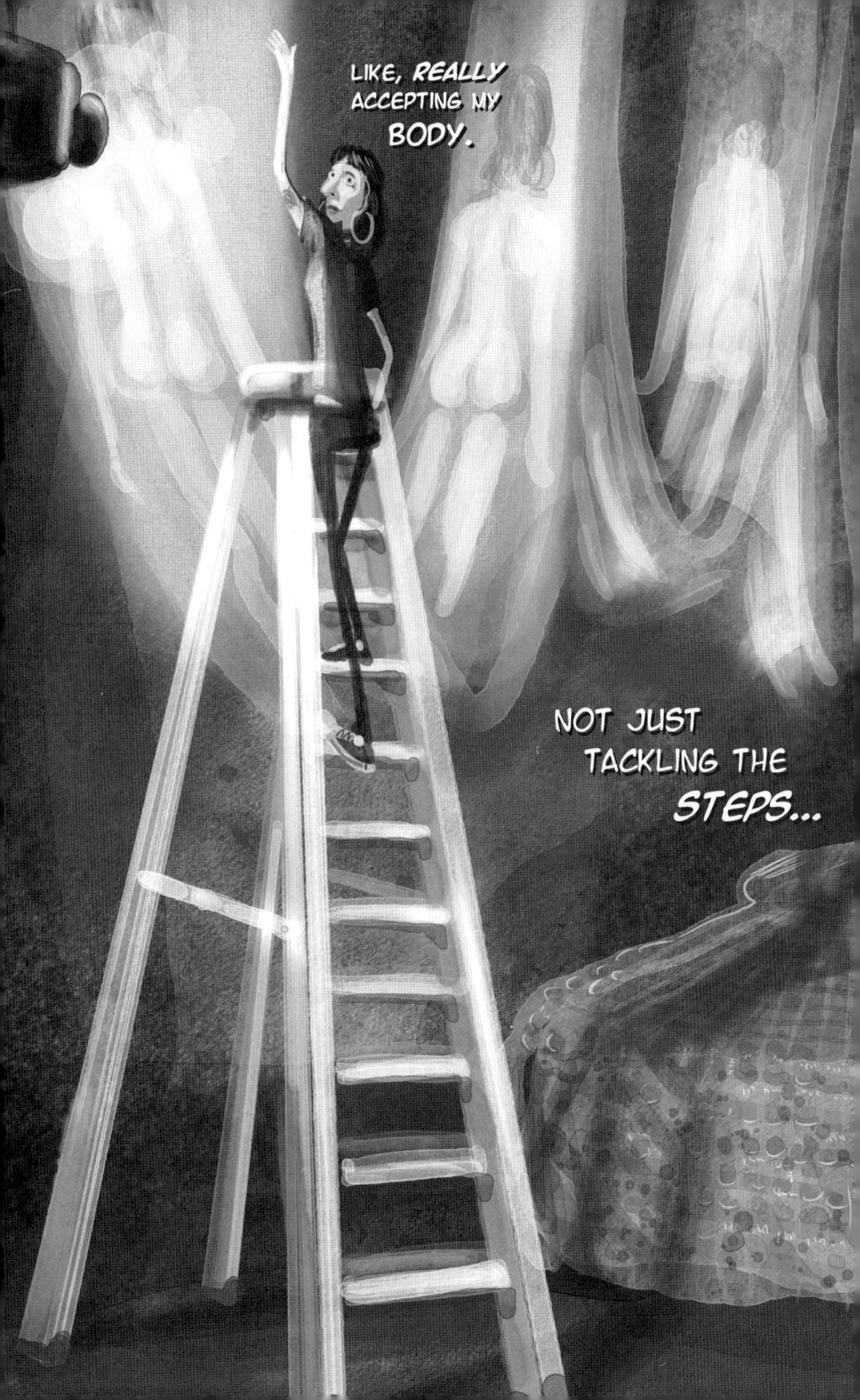

LIKE, REALLY ACCEPTING MY BODY.
NOT JUST TACKLING THE STEPS...

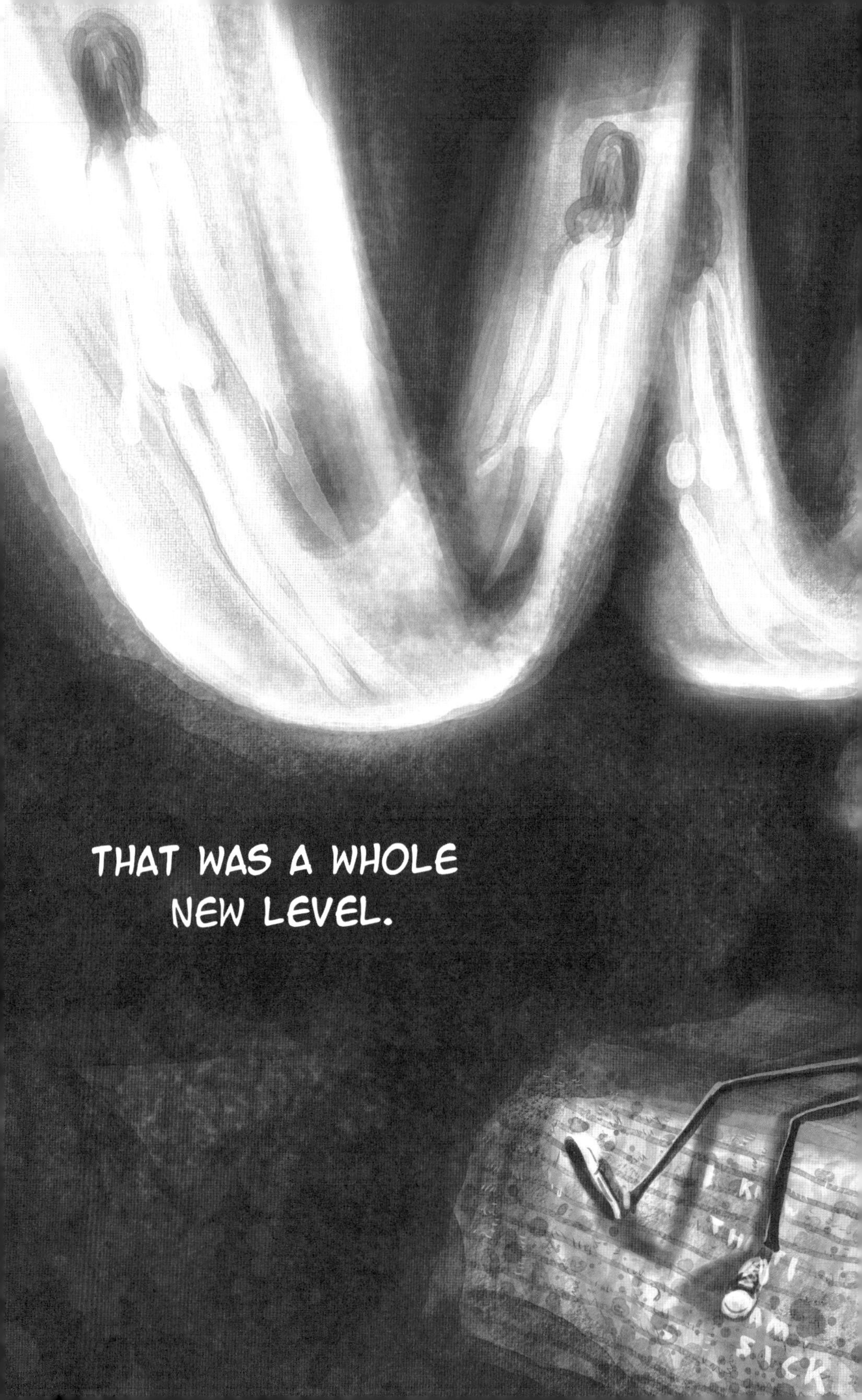
THAT WAS A WHOLE NEW LEVEL.

Chapter 6

WHEN I THINK BACK TO THE TIME OF MY COLLEGE GRADUATION—
IT'S ALMOST LIKE...
I WASN'T THERE.

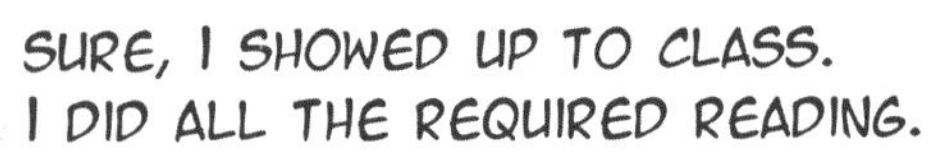
SURE, I SHOWED UP TO CLASS. I DID ALL THE REQUIRED READING.

I EVEN RAISED MY HAND EVERY ONCE IN A WHILE.

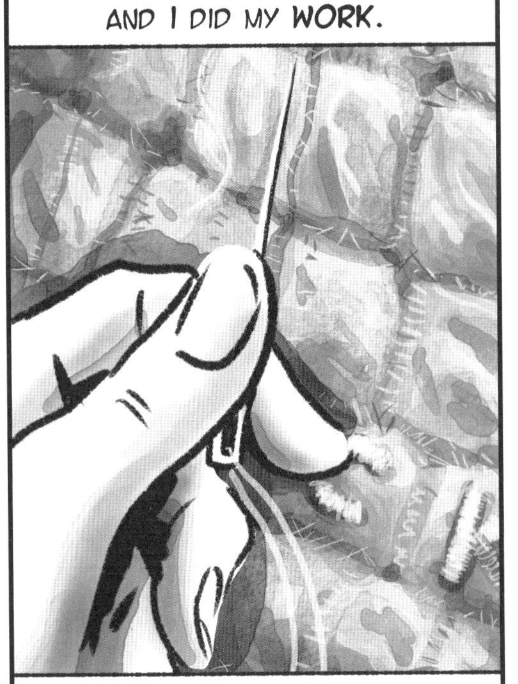
AND I DID MY WORK.
I SPENT HOUR AFTER HOUR MAKING MILLIONS OF TINY STITCHES.

IT'S KIND OF EFFED UP—
BLA! BLAH BLA
BASICALLY ALL I REMEMBER FROM BACK THEN ARE THE MEETINGS.

COUNTLESS, ENDLESS MEETINGS.

OH JEEZ...
BLA BLAH BLA
...HERE WE GO AGAIN.

MEETINGS THAT WERE QUITE HONESTLY WEARING THIN.

I WAS STILL TALKING THROUGH THE STEPS WITH MY SPONSOR...

ANY PROGRESS WITH STEP TEN?
UH...
...SURE.
NOPE.

...BUT I WASN'T REALLY CLIMBING ANY NEW ONES.

YOU'D THINK THAT PREPARING FOR MY THESIS SHOW—

THE PITCHER IN THE WHEAT

H.R PALINGER

AND MY REQUIRED **ORAL DEFENSE**—

WOULD FEEL, WELL, **BIGGER.**

THE CULMINATION OF FOUR YEARS OF INTENSE FOCUS.

BUT I COULDN'T SHAKE THE FEELING THAT I HAD GIVEN MY ART—AND SO MUCH MORE OF MY "REAL LIFE"—THE SHORT SHRIFT.

I WANTED MY WORK TO STAND AS A CELEBRATION OF MY ACCOMPLISHMENTS.

BUT WHEN IT WAS ALL HUNG UP FOR THE FIRST TIME...

ALL I COULD THINK ABOUT...

CONGRATS, LACY.

THE SHOW LOOKS GREAT!

WERE THE HOLES IT REPRESENTED.

THE PITCHE
IN THE WHE
HR. PALINGER
BUT I DONT KNOW WHAT TO SAY
I KNOW THAT I AM SICK

I HAD WORKED SO HARD TO GET TO THIS POINT...
IN MY STUDIO, AND IN CHURCH BASEMENTS...
I KNOW WHAT I AM SICK

BUT STILL I FELT NO *SATISFACTION.*
BUT I DON'T KNOW WHAT TO SAY

YES YOU CA
NOTHING ON THE WALLS COULD GIVE ME BACK THE TIME I HAD SPENT STRUGGLING.
I HAD ALREADY BEEN ACCEPTED TO MY TOP CHOICE MFA PROGRAM...

BUT NOW I JUST WANTED TO GET AWAY.
LACY, HEY GIRL—
NOT NOW.
I NEED TO GET READY.

I WANTED TO GET AWAY FROM ALL OF MY **BODY ISSUES** AND AWAY FROM **PORTLAND'S RAIN** AND ITS ASSOCIATION TO MY **SICKNESS.** I WANTED TO BE FAR, **FAR** AWAY FROM ALL THE **PEOPLE** WHO HAD WATCHED ME **WASTE AWAY,** GETTING *SICKER* AND **SICKER,** BUT NEVER SAID A *WORD* ABOUT IT. AND EVEN THOUGH TIME HAD PASSED, I WANTED TO BE **LIGHT-YEARS** AWAY FROM EVEN THE **POSSIBILITY** OF RUNNING INTO **HENRY.**

BUT BEFORE I COULD MAKE MY ESCAPE...

...I NEEDED TO DEFEND ALL I HAD MADE—
AND ALL I HAD DONE...
UM...
HI.

IN FRONT OF A JURY OF MY MENTORS, PEERS...
EXIT
MY NAME IS LACY DAVIS.
...AND ONE FRIEND.
I'M A THESIS CANDIDATE IN THE INTERMEDIA DEPARTMENT.

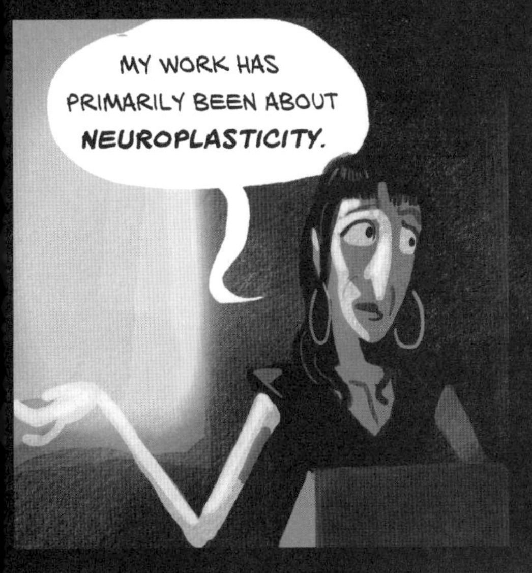

MY WORK HAS PRIMARILY BEEN ABOUT **NEUROPLASTICITY.**

THE **NEGATIVE PATTERNS** WE CREATE IN OUR LIVES DUE TO **HABITUAL THOUGHTS...**
...AND THE STEPS WE CAN MAKE TO **TAKE CONTROL** OF THOSE PATTERNS.

WITH EACH STITCH I ATTEMPTED TO THINK OF SOMETHING *POSITIVE.*
TRAINING MYSELF TO THINK **SELF-LOVING** THOUGHTS...

I SHARED MY STORY AS BEST I COULD, IN THE WAY I WAS USED TO. BUT INSTEAD OF A CROWD THAT DEALT WITH SIMILAR ISSUES...
...THEREFORE CARVING NEW NEURAL PATHWAYS.
...IT WAS A GROUP OF SEASONED ***ART CRITICS.***

IN MANY WAYS, MY RECOVERY WAS ON TRIAL.

ANY QUESTIONS?

UH, YEAH.

YOU IN THE FRONT.

THANKS, LACY. YOU'VE DONE SOME REALLY *INTERESTING* WORK...

BUT I HAVE TO ASK.

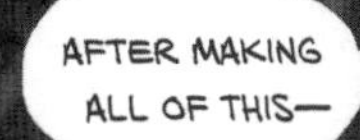

ARE YOU BETTER?

UH.

YEAH!
I MEAN, SURE.
TOTALLY.

AHEM. WELL...
...THAT'S MY TIME.
THANK YOU.

I LEFT IN A DAZE.
TRULY AND COMPLETELY STUMPED.
HEY!

LACY DAVIS!
HEY!
HOLY SHIT, LITTLE BUDDY!

YOU DID IT!
I'M SO PROUD OF YOU, DUDE!

YOU OK?
HOW DID IT FEEL?

SURREAL.

IT WAS ...LIKE MY ENTIRE TIME LIVING IN PORTLAND, VACUUM SEALED.
AND LIKE, I THOUGHT IT WOULD BOTHER ME THAT HENRY WASN'T THERE...
...BUT WHAT BOTHERS ME FOR REAL—
WAS HOW EMPTY IT FELT.

LIKE I'M JUST GOING THROUGH THE MOTIONS WITH...
WITH EVERYTHING.

AND THAT QUESTION!
I MEAN...

AM I BETTER?
LIKE, REALLY?

WHAT IS BETTER?
HMM...

AND THAT RIGHT THERE IS THE **MILLION-DOLLAR QUESTION**!

VERY EXISTENTIAL.

LET ME KNOW WHEN YOU FIGURE IT OUT.

BUT REALLY, I THINK YOU DID GREAT.
AND YOU **ARE** GETTING BETTER.

EVERY DAY!
MAYBE NOT EVERYONE CAN SEE IT...
BUT I CAN!

I MEAN, QUADS AREN'T REBUILT IN A DAY, RIGHT?

YEAH...

...MY SHIT'S LIKE **ROME.**
hrmph!
GIA MAY HAVE BEEN COMFORTABLE WITH THE AMBIGUITY OF WHATEVER "BETTER" MEANT–

BUT I HAD A HARDER TIME LAUGHING IT OFF.
HAHAHAHAHA
IF "BETTER" WASN'T WAITING FOR ME AT THE TOP OF THE 12 STEPS...
WHAT?
WHAT'S SO FUNNY?
THEN WHAT WAS I CLIMBING FOR?

WHAT IS "BETTER" ANYWAY?
(a map to finding out)

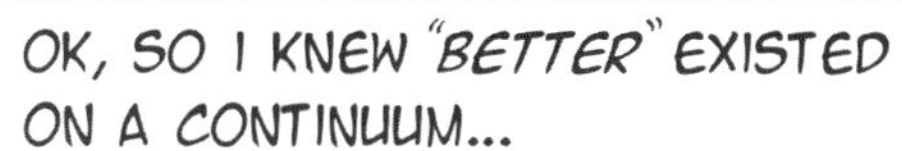

OK, SO I KNEW "BETTER" EXISTED ON A CONTINUUM...

BUT I ALSO THOUGHT THAT IT SHOULD FEEL OBVIOUS WHEN I GOT THERE.

AND WHEN I LOOKED AT THE PLAIN HARD FACTS OF HOW I WAS LIVING—

I KNEW I WASN'T THERE YET.
DESPITE MY WORK ON THE STEPS, I KNEW MY SHIT WAS PRETTY FAR FROM NORMAL.

I STILL WALKED AROUND WITH A *MEASURING SPOON* IN MY BAG—"JUST IN CASE." I STILL EXERCISED *NONSTOP.*

SQUEAK!

SO I STARTED WRITING DOWN WHAT I THOUGHT "BETTER" WOULD LOOK LIKE **FOR ME.**

SEE, THE **STEPS** TOLD ME THINGS *TO DO...*

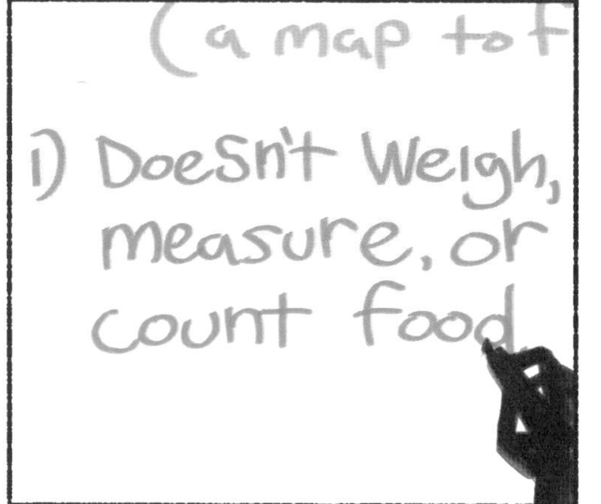

1) Doesn't Weigh, measure, or count food.

BUT NOT WHAT LIFE WOULD LOOK LIKE ON THE OTHER SIDE.

2) Doesn't Spend a lot of time actively thinking about food. (20% of the time?)

AS FAR AS I COULD TELL, IN **OA**...

THERE *WAS* NO OTHER SIDE.

1) Doesn't Weigh, measure, or count food.

STILL, I COULDN'T LEAVE PORTLAND WITHOUT SAYING GOOD-BYE TO MY FAVORITE OA GROUP.
IT WAS A SMALL MEETING, BUT SASKIA WAS THERE, AND JENNIFER. THE FOLKS IN 12-STEPPING WHO I HAD GROWN TO LOVE.
AND I HAD SIGNED UP TO LEAD THIS MEETING *MYSELF*.

ANT ME THE SERENITY TO
I *EVEN* LED THE PRAYER.

AND THEN I TOLD MY STORY IN PORTLAND OA ONE LAST TIME.
YOU GUYS KNOW ME...
I'M LACY.

I DIDN'T SAY ANYTHING **NEW**. THEY HAD **ALL** HEARD A VERSION OF THIS STORY A HUNDRED TIMES ALREADY. BUT I WAS STILL EXPECTING THE INCREDIBLE SENSE OF RELIEF I USUALLY FELT AFTER SHARING MY STRUGGLE.

I WAS SO COLD.

I HAD NO FRIENDS.

I COULDN'T TAKE CARE OF MYSELF.

AND THEN I FOUND THE **MEETINGS.**
I GUESS?

INSTEAD, I FELT STRANGELY ABSENT FROM MY OWN STORY, AND SKEPTICAL OF MY WORDS AS I WAS SPEAKING THEM.

THANK YOU, LACY!
UMM...
YOU'VE INSPIRED US ALL!
DID I EVEN MEAN WHAT I WAS SAYING ANYMORE?

THE BAY WILL BE LUCKY TO HAVE YOU!
Bethany Lutheran Church
GOD PREFERS KIND
ATHEISTS OVER
LATER THAT NIGHT...

...I COULDN'T SLEEP.
I WAS LEAVING FOR SAN FRANCISCO FOR A WHOLE NEW RAIN-FREE LIFE IN THE MORNING.

BUT MY MIND WAS STILL ON OA
AND ONE OF THEIR MOST OFT-REPEATED REFRAINS.

IT WAS SAID THAT WHEN PEOPLE LEFT THE GROUPS...

THEY DIED.
IF I LEFT, WHAT WOULD HAPPEN TO ME?

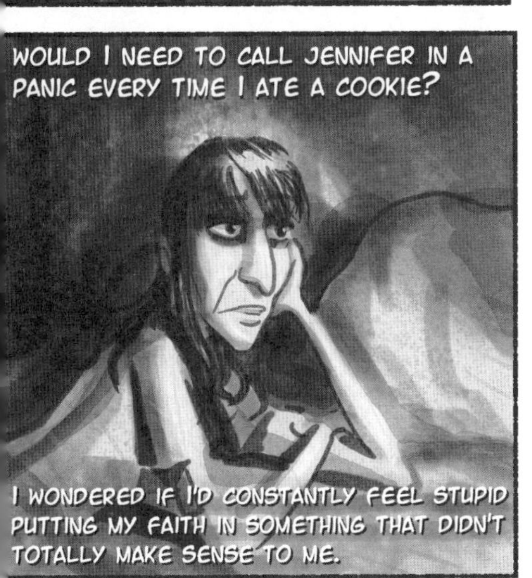
WOULD I NEED TO CALL JENNIFER IN A PANIC EVERY TIME I ATE A COOKIE?
I WONDERED IF I'D CONSTANTLY FEEL STUPID PUTTING MY FAITH IN SOMETHING THAT DIDN'T TOTALLY MAKE SENSE TO ME.

AND IF I EVER FELL IN LOVE AGAIN...
UNLIKELY AS THAT SEEMED AT THE TIME...
SLUMP

HOW WOULD I EXPLAIN OA?

Chapter 7

ONE YEAR LATER...

Weeeee

I DIDN'T PLAN ON LEAVING OA WHEN I MOVED TO CALIFORNIA...
Fisherman
902
IT JUST SORT OF HAPPENED.

I TRIED TO KEEP UP WITH IT...

FOR THE FIRST FEW WEEKS I DUTIFULLY SHOWED UP TO MEETINGS IN SF.

I HESITANTLY ACCEPTED MY **ONE YEAR ABSTINENCE COIN.**
FOR ME, MY ABSTINENCE HAD STARTED THE DAY I DELETED MY CALORIE-TRACKING PROGRAM.

TECHNICALLY I WAS STILL WORKING THE STEPS.
AM I STILL ABSTINENT IF I RUN BEFORE...
AND AFTER LUNCH?
BUT EVER SINCE MY THESIS SHOW, OA FELT LESS LIKE A STAIR CLIMB...

...AND MORE LIKE RUNNING IN CIRCLES.

IT'S NOT LIKE I THOUGHT I WAS **BETTER**...
SWOOSH
...BUT I WAS MUCH, *MUCH* **BUSIER**.

MY NEW **MFA STUDIO** WAS A HILLY EIGHT-MILE RIDE FROM MY TEENSY-TINY DORM ROOM.
OH, YOU'VE GOTTA BE KIDDING ME.
AND BETWEEN MY RIGOROUS **CLASS SCHEDULE**...

...AND MY **"FITNESS" SCHEDULE** ON TOP OF THE COMMUTE...
HUFF
PUFF
HUFF
PUFF
WELL, *SOMETHING* HAD TO GIVE.
IN RETROSPECT, THAT THING *SHOULD* HAVE BEEN THE EXCESSIVE EXERCISE, BUT I WASN'T THERE YET.

WHEN I STARTED GOING TO MY **STUDIO** MORE AND MORE...
AND ATTENDING **OA** LESS AND LESS, THERE WAS NOBODY I KNEW TO CALL ME OUT FOR **BAILING** ON MEETINGS.
I HAD PUT SO MUCH ENERGY INTO TRYING TO BE **RECOVERED** AND **NOW** ALL I REALLY WANTED WAS JUST TO **BE**.
ILLINOIS
22ND ST

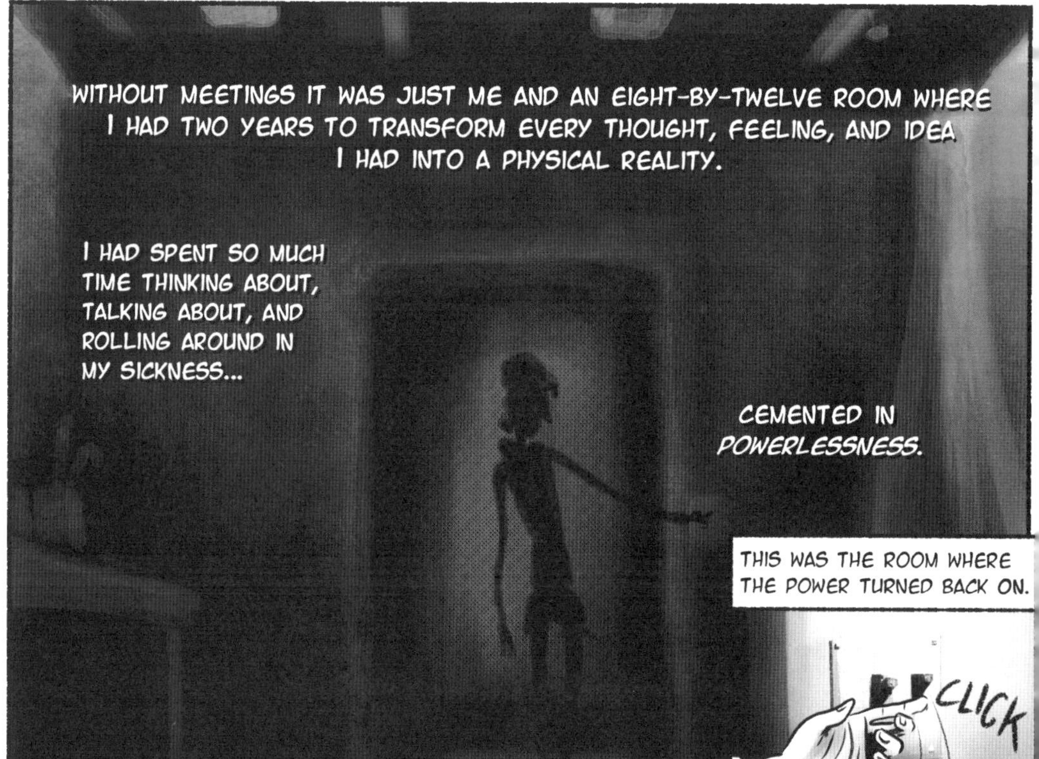
WITHOUT MEETINGS IT WAS JUST ME AND AN EIGHT-BY-TWELVE ROOM WHERE I HAD TWO YEARS TO TRANSFORM EVERY THOUGHT, FEELING, AND IDEA I HAD INTO A PHYSICAL REALITY.
I HAD SPENT SO MUCH TIME THINKING ABOUT, TALKING ABOUT, AND ROLLING AROUND IN MY SICKNESS...
CEMENTED IN *POWERLESSNESS.*
THIS WAS THE ROOM WHERE THE POWER TURNED BACK ON.
CLICK

WHEN IT CAME TO MY RECOVERY, I WAS FINDING THAT RELIVING MY WORST MOMENTS IN A GROUP...
MINE
...COULDN'T HOLD A CANDLE TO THE FEELING OF MOVING FORWARD.

M T W Th F S S
I WANTED NOT ONLY TO RECOVER—
BUT ALSO TO HAVE A **FUCKING LIFE!**

MAKE ART
I SET NEW GOALS FOR MYSELF...
AND WENT AFTER THE
WITH FEROCITY!

I WAS ABLE TO THROW MYSELF INTO MAKING WORK WITHOUT DISTRACTIONS.

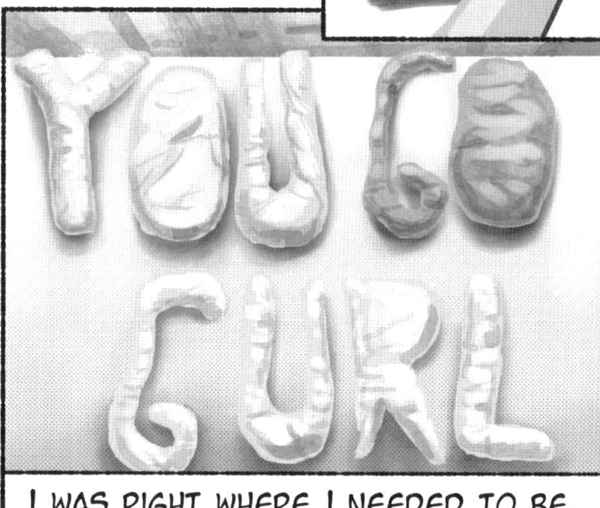

YOU GO
GURL
I WAS RIGHT WHERE I NEEDED TO BE.

THERE WAS NO FOURTH STEP INVENTORY TO TAKE.

THERE WAS NO MEETING THAT I HAD TO ATTEND FOR FEAR OF DEATH.

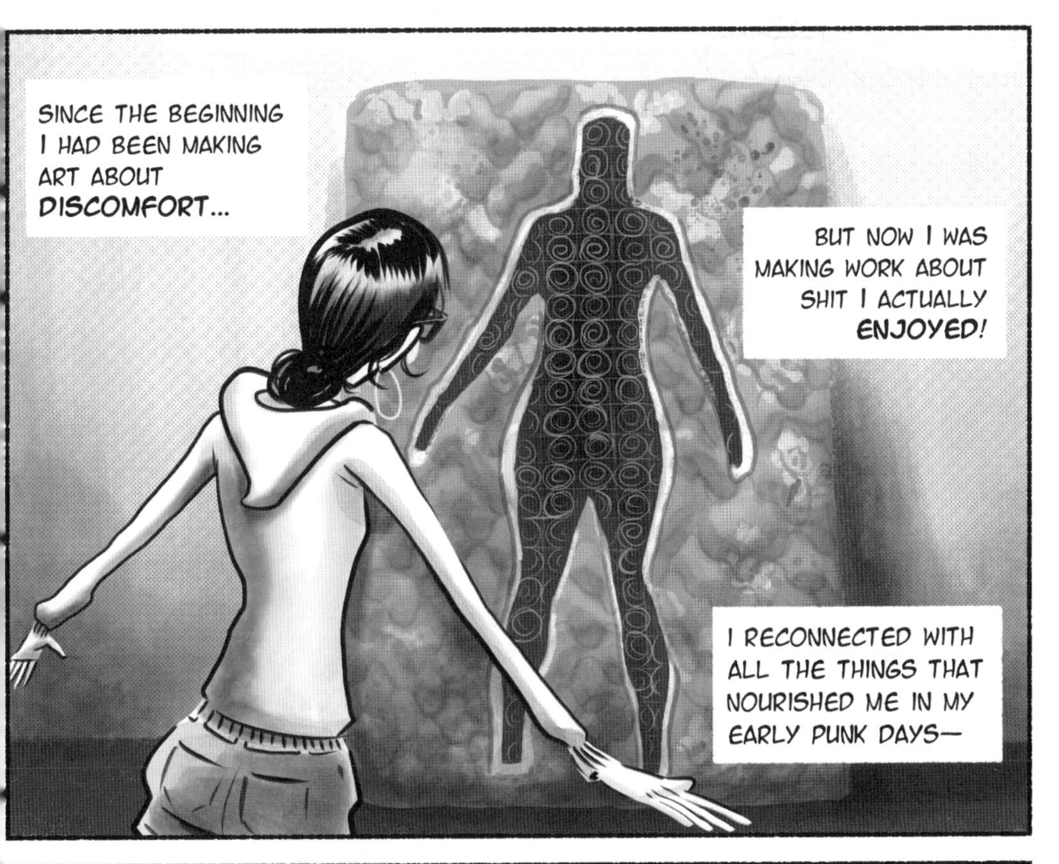
SINCE THE BEGINNING I HAD BEEN MAKING ART ABOUT **DISCOMFORT**...
BUT NOW I WAS MAKING WORK ABOUT SHIT I ACTUALLY **ENJOYED**!
I RECONNECTED WITH ALL THE THINGS THAT NOURISHED ME IN MY EARLY PUNK DAYS—

BOOKS AND MIXTAPES!
THE MORE I MADE ART ABOUT THE THINGS THAT MADE ME **HAPPY**—
THE MORE IT HIGHLIGHTED HOW MUCH OF MYSELF HAD FALLEN AWAY WHEN I FOCUSED ON THE SHIT THAT MADE ME **MISERABLE**.

IT'S KIND OF EVERY PERSON'S DREAM THAT THEY CAN JUST CHANGE LOCATION...
...AND WHATEVER WAS TROUBLING THEM WILL MAGICALLY GET BETTER.

OA SPECIFICALLY WARNED AGAINST ASSUMING A NEW HOME = A NEW LIFE.

12-STEPPERS CALL THIS "PULLING A GEOGRAPHIC" AND INSISTED THAT IT NEVER **EVER** WORKED.

I KNEW ALL THIS, OF COURSE...

...BUT COZY INSIDE THE BOOK NOOK I HAD BUILT FROM FORAGED SCRAPS AND DISCARDED PAPERBACKS—

I FELT SWEPT UP IN THE COMFORTING FLOW OF UNINTERRUPTED WORK.
I MADE NEW WORK ALL DAY, EVERY DAY.

I WAS CHALLENGED TO PROVE MYSELF IN AN ENVIRONMENT WHERE NOBODY KNEW ME...
INTERESTING.
HMN...
OR KNEW HOW FUCKED UP THINGS HAD GOTTEN FOR ME IN PORTLAND.

SURE, I WAS STILL TOO SKINNY.

BUT NOBODY IN GRAD SCHOOL HAD SEEN ME LOOK LIKE A STRAIGHT-UP *BAG OF BONES*.

NOBODY HAD SEEN ME BREAK DOWN AND CRY IN PUBLIC.

HEY LACY!
YOU WANNA GRAB SOME COFFEE WITH US?

THEY ALL JUST ASSUMED I WAS WELL!

AND AS FAR AS THEY WERE CONCERNED—I WAS!

I WAS READY TO *ACT* AS THOUGH THIS WERE *TRUE*...

...UNTIL IT FINALLY ***WAS***.

SO I STARTED HANGING OUT AGAIN. MAKING THE ROUNDS AT PARTIES AND ART OPENINGS.

I WASN'T MAKING ANY REALLY GREAT FRIENDS THIS WAY, BUT IT KEPT ME **BUSY**.

SO BUSY THAT SKIPPING MY **OA** MEETINGS WAS PRACTICALLY A GIVEN.

BUT WHEN I'D GET HOME FROM A LONG DAY IN THE STUDIO...

...I'D FEEL A FAMILIAR LONELINESS KICK BACK IN.

SO I'D DROWN IT THE FUCK OUT THE BEST WAY I KNEW HOW...

TIP TAP TIP TAP TAP TIP TIP TAP

I KNOW, I KNOW...

WHEN I STARTED FLIRTING WITH **KETT** I COULDN'T HELP BUT NOTICE THE PARALLEL TO HOW I'D KICKED OFF MY RELATIONSHIP WITH **HENRY**.

BUT THIS DUDE WAS VETTED—

KETT WAS GOOD FRIENDS WITH SOME OF MY FAVORITE PEOPLE FROM THE PENNSYLVANIA PUNK SCENE.

AND IT SEEMED LIKE HE WAS A VITAL PART OF THIS CIRCLE OF GOOFY WEIRDOS—NONE OF WHOM HAD A CHURCH-BASEMENT ADDICT VIBE.

HE LOOKED, WELL...**FUN!**

NOT LIKE THE KIND OF PERSON TOO CAUGHT UP IN PERFECTION OR APPEARANCES.

BESIDES, HE WAS *CUTE!*

AND HE LIVED ALL THE WAY IN **PHILADELPHIA**.

IF I THREW A LITTLE BIT OF LONG-DISTANCE FLIRT, WHERE WAS THE HARM?

Kett-Nerd

Hi! My name is Lacy Davis and I think you're the babeliest babe who ever babed.
CLICK
S

IN THE MEANTIME, I CLUNG TIGHTLY TO THE LITTLE VICTORIES—A STEP HERE, A MEAL OUT THERE.

AS THE WEEKS WENT BY, I WORKED HARD.

MAKING SURE I ALWAYS ATE **FULL MEALS**.

WORKING TO NOT ONLY GET BACK TO A STABLE WEIGHT...

THIS IS NOT TOO MUCH FOOD.
THIS IS A TOTALLY NORMAL AMOUNT TO EAT!

BUT A HEALTHY **MIND-SET**.

TWO MORE POUNDS UP!

REWIRING MY NEURONS **IRL** WAS A LOT HARDER THAN EMBROIDERING THEM.

SOMETIMES MY VICTORIES FELT FORCED, BUT I ACCEPTED THAT EVEN THOUGH I WAS PRETTY OVER 12-STEPPING...

I STILL HAD A LOT OF CLIMBING TO DO.

HEY LACY!
SOMEONE SENT YOU ANOTHER PACKAGE...
WHAT??!
OMG!

ROMANCE, ON THE OTHER HAND...

...INSPIRED AN ENTIRELY DIFFERENT REALITY.
REALLY?
IS IT FROM **PHILLY**?
LEMME SEE!
I TAKE IT THIS IS FROM THE **BOY**?

YEAH!
INSTEAD OF FOOD JOURNALS AND DOCTOR'S APPOINTMENTS...

IT WAS LUNCH BOXES PACKED WITH TOYS AND LETTERS AND MIXTAPES!
IT WAS LEGIT EXCITEMENT!

AND IT HAD *ZERO* TO DO WITH MY *WEIGHT*, *EXERCISE*, OR *FOOD*!
I'LL ADMIT MY INITIAL CRUSH ON KETT WAS A WAY TO TEST MY RECOVERY A BIT.
PLOP!
FLIRTING WITH HIM WAS A WAY TO PUSH MY LIMITS WITHOUT HAVING TO COMMIT TO A LOCAL PERSON WHO COULD SEE ALL OF MY WEIRD ROUTINES AND QUIRKS.

BUT AS OUR LETTERS FLEW BACK AND FORTH ACROSS THE COUNTRY...
I THOUGHT MORE AND MORE ABOUT WHAT AN **IRL** SOMETHING COULD BE LIKE.

ON THE SURFACE, KETT HAD A LOT OF THE SAME THINGS GOING FOR HIM AS HENRY.
SMARTY-PANTS
CUTIE FACE
LOTSA TATTOOS
MEGA-TALENT
DRUG FREE
OLD-SCHOOL PUNK STYLE
CRUCIAL SHOES

BUT HIS LETTERS REVEALED SO MUCH MORE!

KETT WAS SILLY.
IN PHILLY IT GETS SO HOT, WE FILL GARBAGE BAGS WITH HOSE WATER AND CHILL IN OUR BACKYARD!
IT'S CALLED "COOL BAGGING."
HE WAS SELF-DEPRECATING.
YOUR NEW WEB COMIC IS SO GOOD!
TAP TAP TAP
TAP TAP TAP
EH, IT'S OK, I GUESS. IT'S ONLY A TWO-PAGER.
I'M NOT GONNA THROW MYSELF A PARADE OR ANYTHING.
HE WAS VEGAN, INTO HEALTH AND FITNESS, BUT NOT OBSESSED WITH ANY OF THAT.
HIGH KNEES
POWER SQUAT
MUMMY KICKS
HE WAS ALWAYS LOOKING FOR WAYS TO IMPROVE HIMSELF AND HIS ART.
TAP TAP TAP TAP TAP TAP
SEND
I JUST THINK I'VE HIT MY LIMIT WITH WEB COMICS...
...AND WITH LIVING IN PHILLY TOO.
SO I'VE BEEN APPLYING TO A BUNCH OF MFA WRITING PROGRAMS.
I WAS HELLA SMITTEN!

SIGH
I'D LAY IN MY DORM BED WONDERING WHAT IT WOULD BE LIKE TO SMOOCH.

I KNEW IT WAS BECOMING MORE THAN JUST INFATUATION, THOUGH. WE HAD RECENTLY STARTED TALKING ON THE PHONE IN ADDITION TO ALL THE LETTERS AND TEXTING.
BA-BA BA-BA Together
868
BORDERLANDS
AND AS I'D WALK AROUND THE CITY, LISTENING TO HIS MIXTAPES, I'D REPLAY OUR CONVERSATIONS.

WHEN I SAW SOMETHING FUNNY OR INTERESTING, I WONDERED WHAT KETT WOULD SAY.
BORDERLANDS BOOKS
BA-BA BA BA BAAA
I WONDERED IF HE'D LIKE SAN FRANCISCO.

MOSTLY, I LIKED THAT SINCE GETTING TO KNOW HIM...
CAFE
SMILES WERE NO LONGER SO HARD TO COME BY.

I'D COME TO COUNT ON HIM FOR THOSE SMILES.
RING RING
SO IT WAS EXTRA SCARY WHEN I DECIDED TO "COME CLEAN" ABOUT MY ED.

SOME OF MY LETTERS HAD KINDA DANCED AROUND IT.
CLICK

DAVIS!
WHAT'S UP?

I'D *HINTED,* SURE, BUT I HAD NEVER REVEALED HOW BAD IT GOT.
OH, NOTHING. JUST TAKING A PIT STOP AT **DOLORES PARK.**
UM, YOUR NEW TAPE IS REALLY GOOD.
BUT I COULDN'T JUST HINT FOREVER.

OF COURSE I TRIED TO STALL.
UH, WHAT ARE YOU UP TO?
OH, THE **USUAL...**

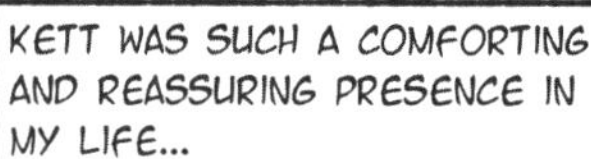
KETT WAS SUCH A COMFORTING AND REASSURING PRESENCE IN MY LIFE...

...AND EVEN FROM ACROSS THE COUNTRY...
...DRAWING COMICS!
AND LISTENING TO YOUR LATEST MIXTAPE.
WHICH RIPS, BY THE WAY.
COOL, COOL...
...HE WAS PRETTY GOOD AT READING ME.

HEY, IS EVERYTHING OK?
SCRATCH
YOU SOUND KINDA STRESSED.

YEAH, YEAH.
I'M OK.
IT'S JUST...
SO MUCH FOR *STALLING.*

YOU KNOW IN MY LETTER, WHEN I TALKED ABOUT THAT **FOOD AND BODY** STUFF?

SURE, YEAH.
YEAH, WELL...

IT ACTUALLY GOT PRETTY BAD AT ONE POINT.
OK...
YEAH...

AND, LIKE, I'M DOING BETTER. LIKE, A LOT. BUT YOU SHOULD PROBABLY KNOW THAT I STILL GO TO 12-STEP MEETINGS AND STUFF...
BUT I PROMISE I'M NOT A FREAK. I DON'T, LIKE, BELIEVE IN GOD OR ANYTHING. I'M DOING BETTER!

I WAS REALLY SCARED. WHAT IF HE WANTED TO PEACE THE FUCK OUT?
NO MORE LETTERS. NO MORE MIXTAPES...

NO MORE OUT-OF-NOWHERE SMILES.

HELLO?
I'M HERE...

LACY, LISTEN...IT'S OK. REALLY!
AND DON'T FREAK...

BUT I KIND OF ALREADY GUESSED.
YOU DID!?
WELL, BETWEEN YOUR LETTERS...

...AND SOME OF YOUR OLDER PICTURES ON FACEBOOK...
GRRRRR FACEBOOK!
NO, IT'S OK.

LOOK, LACY... UM, I REALLY LIKE YOU. AND DUH, I KNOW THAT RECOVERING FROM ADDICTION TAKES TIME...
BUT THANKS FOR TELLING ME...

AND YOU KNOW THAT IF YOU EVER NEED TO TALK ABOUT YOUR FOOD STUFF... YOU CAN TOTALLY CALL ME.
YOU'RE NOT LIKE SUPER GROSSED OUT?
WHAT?

OF COURSE NOT!
JEEZ! I'D NEVER JUDGE SOMEONE FOR BEING SICK!
HOW FUCKED UP WOULD THAT BE?

SO, LIKE...WE CAN STILL BE PEN PALS?
ARE YOU FUCKING KIDDING ME??

I CAN'T WAIT TO GET THE CHANCE TO MAKE OUT!
KETTNER!
SO BOLD!
OH, PUH-LEAZE!

WE'VE BEEN SENDING EACH OTHER CUTE-ASS LETTERS AND MIXTAPES FOR MONTHS.
WE TALK ALMOST EVERY DAY NOW.
I MEAN, GIVE ME SOME CREDIT, DAVIS...

DID YOU REALLY THINK I DIDN'T KNOW WE WERE FLIRTING?
WELL, NOW THAT WE CLEARED THAT UP...

...TELL ME MORE ABOUT MAKING OUT.

THE EVENTUAL EPIC MAKE-OUT DID END UP HAPPENING—
SOONER THAN EXPECTED.

C'MON.
C'MON.
PICK UP!
HELLO?
LACY?
HEY!
THIS TIME IT WAS KETT WHO MADE THE CALL...

DID I CATCH YOU AT A BAD TIME?
WHAT?
NO, I'M JUST WORKING IN MY STUDIO.
WHAT'S UP?

WELL, I JUST GOT HOME AND...I GOT MY **LETTER** FROM **CCA**.
I'M **FREAKING** OUT.

I...I **GOT IN**.
I STILL GOTTA SORT OUT *FINANCIAL AID* AND STUFF...
BUT I SHOULD BE MOVING TO THE BAY IN SEPTEMBER.

I'D SPENT A RIDICULOUS AMOUNT OF TIME DAYDREAMING ABOUT KETT, BUT ZERO TIME WITH HIM IN PERSON...

I NEEDED TO KNOW IF THIS DUDE WAS AS GREAT AS HE SEEMED ON PAPER, AND I NEEDED TO KNOW BEFORE HE LANDED IN MY CITY.
YOU STILL THERE?
TOTALLY.
THAT'S GREAT, KETT. CONGRATS!
BUT TELL ME...
WHAT'S YOUR AUGUST LOOKING LIKE?

THERE WAS ONLY ONE WAY TO FIND OUT.

I GOT INTO PHILADELPHIA AFTER TEN HOURS OF DELAYED FLIGHTS AND THREE TRANSFERS.

I WAS SHAKING IN MY SLIP-ON VANS. I HAD GRABBED A COPY OF **SKY MALL**, WHICH I BRANDISHED LIKE A SHIELD.

LACY!
OVER HERE!

I SHOULDN'T HAVE BEEN WORRIED.
RIGHT AWAY, KETT FELT...
...WELL, **RIGHT**.

THIS IS *NICE*, HUH?
YEAH...
...IT *IS*.

NOT THAT I WASN'T STILL *NERVOUS*.
LOOK, IT'S A THREE-FOOT-TALL YODA STATUE THAT TELLS FORTUNES LIKE A MAGIC 8-BALL...
UM... COOL?

AND I WASN'T THE ONLY ONE.
CAN I HOLD YOUR HAND?
SURE...

CAN I TELL YOU ABOUT THE TIME MY TOOTH BROKE OFF WHILE I WAS EATING A BAGEL?
OOOO-KAY?

WELL, I HAD A ROOT CANAL HERE, SEE?
MY TEETH ARE THE WORST...
UH-HUH...

AND THEN...
UM...
...YOU KNOW WHAT?

WHAT AM I DOING?
THERE'S A BEAUTIFUL GIRL IN MY BED AND I'M TELLING DENTAL HORROR STORIES!

WE SHOULD PROBABLY JUST MAKE OUT...
YES PLEASE!

DESPITE KETT'S REPELLING DENTISTRY TALES, WE MADE OUT UNTIL SUNRISE.
I KNEW, BY HOW COMFORTABLE I FELT, THAT—THIS WAS REAL PUNK-ROCK LOVE!

THE NEXT MORNING WE WOKE STILL TIGHTLY SPOONED.
WOW, THAT NEVER HAPPENS!
I KNOW. WE SNUG PRETTY GOOD!
SUPER GOOD!
COFFEE?
YES!

BUT BEFORE WE COULD PROPERLY CAFFEINATE...
YOU SEEING WHAT I'M SEEING?
HELL YEAH!

BOUNCE HOUSE!

THIS WAS THE KIND OF FUN I IMAGINED KETT HAD ALL THE TIME.
GO TEAM!
THE KIND OF CAREFREE FUN I HADN'T EXPERIENCED SINCE WAY BEFORE OA.
THE KIND OF FUN I'D BEEN MISSING.

Chapter 8

THAT SEPTEMBER, KETT MOVED INTO MY TINY DORM ROOM ON GEARY STREET IN DOWNTOWN SAN FRANCISCO.

TECHNICALLY I WAS BREAKING THE RULES, SNEAKING HIM PAST SECURITY EVERY DAY...

WHAT CHAPPY ARE YOU UP TO?

...WE WERE STILL **PUNKS** AFTER ALL, EVEN IF WE WERE PURSUING ADVANCED DEGREES.

FIVE.
AH, YOU'RE BEATING ME.

IT'S NO EXAGGERATION TO SAY THAT DESPITE THE TIGHT QUARTERS, WE WERE EXPERIENCING WHAT SOME REAL GROWN-UPS MIGHT CALL "**DOMESTIC BLISS.**"

I'M A FAST READER, DUDE!

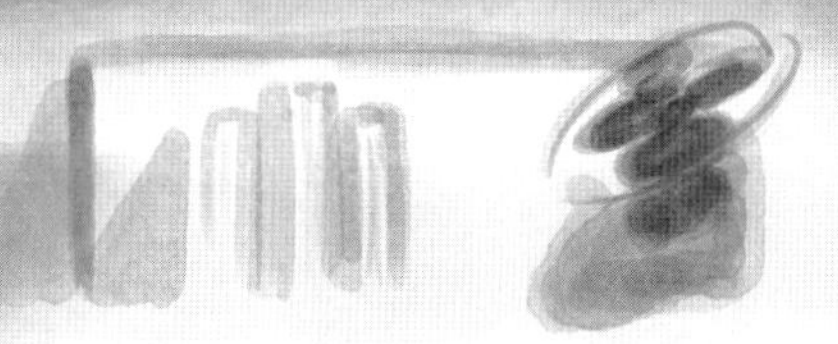

IT WAS ALSO A CRASH COURSE IN LEARNING EACH OTHER'S QUIRKS.

I NEED TO DROP A DEUCE.
KNOCK YOURSELF OUT, MY DOG.

LIKE, FOR INSTANCE, THE LENGTHS WE WOULD GO TO TO GET SOME *ALONE TIME.*

SLAM
KETT WAS FOND OF HOUR-LONG POOPS...

AAAAH!
YOU HAVE FUN IN THERE, NERD?
I FEEL TEN POUNDS LIGHTER!
OR IN MY CASE...

...THE LENGTHS I WOULD GO TO GET A WORKOUT IN.
WELL, OUR PLANE IS AT SEVEN IN THE MORNING...
SO I'LL SET THE ALARM FOR 3:45...

THAT WAY WE CAN **AT LEAST** GO ON A QUICK RUN.
UUUUUHHHH...
WHAT?

WHEN YOU HAVE A SUPEREARLY FLIGHT, IT'S OK TO SKIP EXERCISE, DUDE.
AND WE HAVE SUCH A PACKED DAY TOMORROW TOO. IT JUST DOESN'T MAKE SENSE, YA KNOW?

FINE!
WHATEVER!
I'LL JUST RUN BY MYSELF!

SLAM

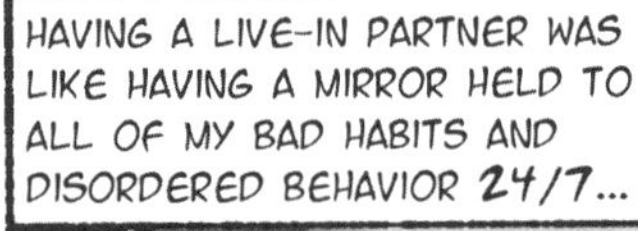
HAVING A LIVE-IN PARTNER WAS LIKE HAVING A MIRROR HELD TO ALL OF MY BAD HABITS AND DISORDERED BEHAVIOR 24/7...

HEY.
IT'S OK.

...WHICH WASN'T ALWAYS MY FAVORITE...
I'M SORRY.
I'M JUST SO USED TO MY ROUTINES.

...BUT IT DID KEEP ME ACCOUNTABLE IN A WAY OA NEVER COULD.
I'M THE WORST!
NO, NO!
YOU'RE MY FAVORITE!
WHEN I ACTED OUT, I SAW HOW IT AFFECTED THE PERSON I CARED FOR THE MOST.
IT'S GONNA BE ALL RIGHT!
I WAS MAKING REAL STRIDES WITH MY ED. I WASN'T WEIGHING AND MEASURING MY FOOD ANYMORE, BUT I WAS NERVOUS...

I'M JUST EXTRA SCARED ABOUT GOING BACK!
I KNOW, KID.
WE WERE ABOUT TO VISIT PORTLAND FOR THE FIRST TIME SINCE I HAD MOVED.

AND, IT WAS MY BIRTHDAY.
I HAD WANTED IT TO BE A KIND OF HOMECOMING PARTY, BUT IT WAS WEIRD.
WEIRD TO BE BACK WALKING THE SAME STREETS I HAD WHEN I WAS AT MY SICKEST.
THE SAME STREETS I HAD WALKED WITH HENRY.
POWELL'S
USED & NEW BOO
STILL, I WAS DETERMINED THAT TWENTY-EIGHT WAS GOING TO BE MY BEST YEAR YET. I WAS GONNA LEAVE ALL THIS ED STUFF IN THE DUST, AND I WANTED TO CELEBRATE.

OF COURSE, I MAY HAVE BITTEN OFF MORE THAN I COULD CHEW.
HEY, HOW ARE YOU HOLDING UP?
OK...
NERVOUS...
IT'LL BE ALL RIGHT...
KETT WAS RIGHT BY MY SIDE THE WHOLE TIME, OFFERING ENCOURAGEMENT AND SUPPORT.

BUT, YOU KNOW WE CAN TOTALLY *BAIL* IF THIS IS TOO ROUGH.
NO, IT'S COOL...
WHICH WAS A GOOD THING...

CAUSE I NEEDED BACKUP.
...BUT STICK CLOSE.

LACY DAVIS!

I HADN'T SEEN MOST OF THESE FACES SINCE I'D LEFT PORTLAND FOR GRAD SCHOOL...
I SAVED YOU A SEAT!
...AND IN THAT TIME MY BODY HAD *CHANGED*.

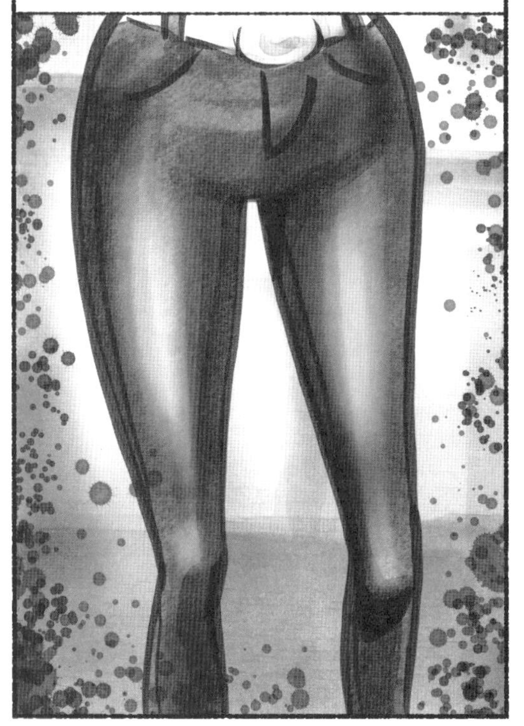
WERE THEY NOTICING THE WAY MY **THIGHS** HAD GROWN?

OR THE CHUBBINESS OF MY **CHEEKS**?

GULP.
I WAS PAINFULLY AWARE OF ALL THEIR EYEBALLS ON ME.
DEEP BREATH.

I HAD WORKED SO HARD TO LET MY BODY GET BETTER, BUT THE *BAD THOUGHTS...*
THEY STILL *BUBBLED.*

EVEN WHEN I WAS ABLE TO SHAKE THEM OFF...
THEY WAITED IN EVERY SILENT MOMENT.

HEY!
EARTH TO LACY.
WHICH WAS HARDER TO HIDE WITH PEOPLE WHO ACTUALLY KNEW ME.
I WAS JUST SAYING YOU SHOULD HUDDLE UP WITH YOUR DUDE!
ASSEMBLING THIS GET-TOGETHER WAS AS MUCH A TEST AS IT WAS A PARTY.

'CAUSE I BROUGHT MY TRUSTY POLAROID!
AN "I'M REALLY OK, I'M REALLY BETTER" TEST.

CHEEK TO CHEEK, Y'ALL!
I REALLY WANTED TO SHOW EVERYONE I WASN'T SICK, WHETHER I BELIEVED THAT WAS TRUE OR NOT.

NOW SAY, HAPPY BIRTHDAY!

THERE YOU GO.
COUPLE OF CUTIES.

NOW...
...WHICH OF YOUR BIRTHDAYS IS IT AGAIN?

WHAT DO YOU MEAN?
IT'S **MINE.**
YOU OK?

OH YEAH...I WAS JUST **KIDDING.**
I KNEW THAT...
AND HOW OLD ARE YOU NOW?

TWENTY-EIGHT!
JESUS!

WE'RE, LIKE, ALL OFFICIALLY OLD AND MOLDY.
TELL ME ABOUT IT.

EVEN IF GIA WAS ACTING A LITTLE *OFF*, I WAS STILL FOCUSED ON PASSING THE *FINAL TEST*...

AT LEAST WE HAVE **DESSERT.**

BIRTHDAY MILKSHAKE!
WHOOOOO!!!
HAPPY BIRTHDAY
THERE IT WAS...

MY FINAL EXAM.
A VEGAN CHOCOLATE SHAKE WITH WHIPPED TOPPING, AND CACAO FLAKES, FESTOONED WITH SPARKLERS.
MAKE A WISH, DUFUS!

A WISH?
IN SOME WAYS I HAD EVERYTHING I WANTED.
I WAS SURROUNDED BY GOOD FRIENDS.
HAD A RAD ROMANTIC DUDE-FRIEND WHO MADE ME FEEL AMAZING.
BUT STILL...
I WISHED DRINKING A MILKSHAKE COULD JUST BE...
...EASY.
BUT NOT EVERY WISH COULD COME TRUE.
I JUST HAD TO DO MY BEST.

NOT LETTING THE DARK THOUGHTS IN.

IGNORING THE FEELING OF EVERYONE'S **EYES** ON MY EATING.

AND IF I COULD MANAGE ALL THAT...

MAYBE I COULD *ACTUALLY* RECOVER INSTEAD OF JUST PLAYING THE PART.

WELL, WELL, WELL...
LOOK AT YOU WITH THAT SHAKE!
DUDE! THAT'S LIKE, **HUGE!**

I JUST WANT YOU TO KNOW, LIKE, I **SEE** YOU *HANDLING* THAT SHIT!
YOU'RE DOING GREAT!

I'M **SUPERPROUD** OF YOU!
HIGH-FIVE, SISTER!
THANKS, G!

YOU'VE GOT ANOTHER GRADUATION COMING UP TOO, HUH?
YEP! NEXT MONTH!
SO WHAT'S NEXT FOR YOU GUYS?

WELL, I'M ABOUT TO HAVE A MASTER'S DEGREE IN "NEW GENRES"...
SO THE *POSSIBILITIES* ARE **FUCKIN' ENDLESS.**
HA!
WE DO HAVE A PRETTY COOL PLAN FOR THE SUMMER ,THOUGH.

THAT'S RIGHT! ME AND KETT ARE GONNA DO AN **APARTMENT SWAP** WITH SOME EAST COAST BUDDIES!
YEAH, WE'LL BE LIVING IT UP IN *LUXURIOUS* **SOUTH PHILLY!**
OH YEAH?

I'VE ACTUALLY BEEN THINKING ABOUT GETTING OUTTA HERE TOO!
PORTLAND HAS BEEN *KINDA* ROUGH LATELY.
I WAS GONNA GIVE **NYC** ANOTHER TRY.

THAT **RULES!**
KETT'S *BIASED*, THOUGH. HE'S FROM NEW YORK.
WOW! SO **EAST COAST** HERE WE COME!

WE GOTTA CAPTURE THIS MOMENT!
HUDDLE IN!

CHAPTER 9

PHILADELPHIA, 2012
PHILLY WAS A BIG ADJUSTMENT FOR THIS WEST COAST KID...
HONK HONK HONK
GET OUTTA THA' WAY, YA HUMP!
FOR THE FIRST COUPLE WEEKS OF SUMMER, KETT AND I SURFED THE COUCH OF...

...DISGRACELAND—AN INFAMOUS SOUTH PHILLY PUNK HOUSE WHERE WE WERE SURROUNDED BY SOME OF KETT'S BEST FRIENDS IN THE WORLD.

RISE AND SHINE NERDS!
YES!
WAKE UP AND LIVE!
KETT WAS HAPPY TO BE BACK IN HIS ELEMENT.
WHA...?
AND I TOOK THE OPPORTUNITY TO PRACTICE NORMALCY...

WANNA HIT UP THE COMIC BOOK STORE?
EVEN IF THE ENVIRONMENT WAS TOTALLY FOREIGN TO ME.
MOS DEF!
I'M NOT DOING ANYTHING BEFORE COFFEE!
DIIIIIIIIIID SOMEONE SAY COFFEE?
IT WAS REALLY CHALLENGING TO BE AROUND SO MANY PEOPLE ALL THE TIME.

SEE, PHILLY PUNKS HAVE THE MAGICAL ABILITY TO HANG OUT AS A FULL-TIME JOB.

WALL SIT AT RITTENHOUSE!
SWIM CLUB AT SIX, THOUGH!
AND PINK COFFINS ARE PLAYING TONIGHT.

AFTER GRAD SCHOOL ON RELATIONSHIP ISLAND, THIS MUCH SOCIALIZING WAS KIND OF A CULTURE SHOCK.

THERE WERE SUDDENLY LOTS OF PEOPLE AROUND TO, SAY, HAVE VHS MOVIE NIGHTS WITH.

PEOPLE TO TAKE ME SWIMMING.

PEOPLE TO WORK OUT WITH.

THREE—TWO—
ONE—
POWER JUMPS!
GO!!!

AND, PEOPLE TO **EAT** WITH...

DIG IN, EVERYBODY!
VEGAN TOT-CHOS!

I **WANTED** THE NORMALIZATION OF FOOD AND FITNESS.

BUT EVERY NEW DYNAMIC, EVERY CHANGE IN ROUTINE...

FELT LIKE A THREAT TO MY SURVIVAL.

NO MORE TOT
RUN IT OFF

I WAS CONSTANTLY PAUSING IN HANG-OUTS TO EXPUNGE NEGATIVE THOUGHTS, WHICH FRUSTRATED ME TERRIBLY.

HEY!
WHA?
EARTH TO LACY!

RAMSEY WAS JUST TALKING ABOUT ONE OF YOUR FAVORITE TOPICS...
WORKING OUT!
OH.
SORRY, I WAS ZONING OUT.

IT'S COOL. I WAS JUST SAYING HOW I'VE GOTTEN REALLY INTO LIFTING WEIGHTS LATELY...
IT'S KINDA BLOWING MY MIND.
I'VE SERIOUSLY GOTTEN SO MUCH STRONGER IN JUST A FEW MONTHS.
COOL!

YOU GUYS SHOULD GIVE IT A TRY!
I'D BE DOWN.
EH.
I'LL JUST STICK TO CARDIO.
I WAS PRETTY SURE THAT LIFTING WEIGHTS LED TO BIGGER BODIES—

WEIGHT LIFTING?
SHUDDERR
NOT MY THING.

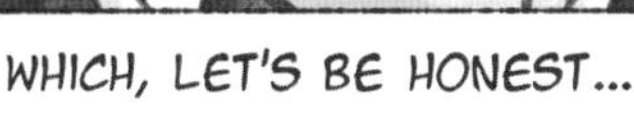
WHICH, LET'S BE HONEST...

I WAS NOT READY FOR.

MAN, RAMSEY IS SO COOL!
AND HER COMICS ARE GREAT!
MOST DEFINITELY.
GRINDCORE HOUSE VEGAN
BUT SPEAKING OF...

WHY'D YOU GET SO WEIRD WHEN SHE MENTIONED **WEIGHT LIFTING**?
I WASN'T BEING **WEIRD**...
I DIDN'T **WANT** TO BE ACTING *WEIRD*...

BUT I KNEW I HAD GOTTEN A LITTLE FREAKED.

WELLLL...
YEAH, YOU KINDA WERE.
LOOK, THERE'S NOTHING WRONG WITH MY WORKOUTS. I LIKE THEM AS THEY ARE.
BURNING FEWER CALORIES...

AND BUILDING MORE *MASS*...
BUT AREN'T YOU ALWAYS SAYING YOU **DON'T LIKE** YOUR RELATIONSHIP WITH EXERCISE AS IT IS?
MAYBE IT'S TIME TO TRY SOMETHING **DIFFERENT**.
DID ***NOT*** SEEM APPEALING.

LOOK, MAYBE I WILL TRY IT, EVENTUALLY.
...BUT I DON'T WANT TO END UP LOOKING LIKE A **SHE-HULK**!
IS THAT WHAT YOU WANT?
LACY, BABE...
I DON'T CARE **WHAT** YOU LOOK LIKE.
EVEN WITHOUT MUCH OF AN EATING PROBLEM SETTING ME BACK ANYMORE...

I **LOVE** YOU, DUDE.
I JUST WANT YOU TO BE **HAPPY** AND **HEALTHY**.
WHATEVER...
MY **THINKING PROBLEM** WAS STARING ME RIGHT IN THE FACE.

BUT I WASN'T READY TO STARE BACK.

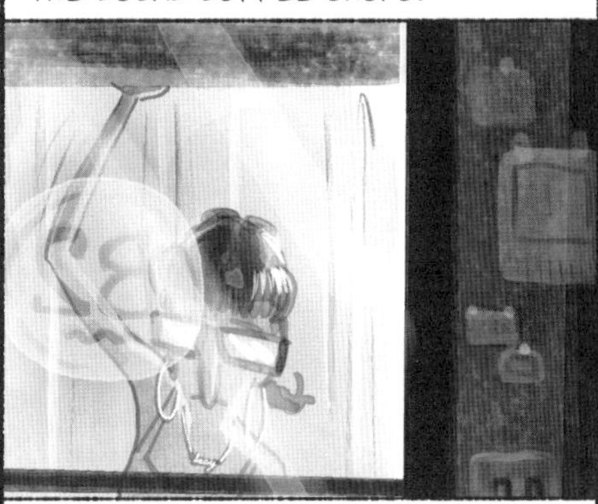
I SCORED A SUMMER JOB AT ONE OF THE LOCAL COFFEE SHOPS.
IT WAS MY FIRST JOB IN THE SERVICE INDUSTRY.

IT WAS ALSO MY **LAST**.
GOOD MORNING!
LOOKS LIKE YOU'RE THE FIRST CUSTOMER OF THE DAY!

WHAT CAN I GET FOR YOU TODAY?

?

UH...

I'M NOT SURE WHAT YOU WA—
BLACK COFFEE
SAME AS ALWAYS.

OH.
OK.
LEARN TO USE YOUR WORDS, ASSHOLE.
POUR
THERE WAS A LEARNING CURVE, BOTH IN THE WAYS OF THE INDUSTRY...

AND IN ACCLIMATING TO EAST COAST PERSONALITIES.
GRUNT
GRUMBLE
SWIPE
YEESH!

BETWEEN THE CONSTANT HANG-OUTS...
AND THE CROWDED CAFÉ...
I WAS FEELING HELLA BURNT OUT.
THANKFULLY, KETT REMINDED ME THAT THERE WAS ALWAYS ONE PLACE I COULD COUNT ON FOR A MOMENT OF QUIET.
BUT EVEN WHEN THE WORLD AROUN ME WAS SILENCED.

...MY BRAIN GOT **LOUD**.
YOUR BOSS HATES YOU
THOSE ARE KETT'S FRIENDS NOT YOURS!
YOU'RE GETTING BIG!
LISTENING TO THE VOICES IN MY HEAD WAS **EXHAUSTING**.
OU'RE NOT OING ANYTHING ITH YOUR LIFE!
YOU'RE NOT MAKING ART
GETTING FAT
KETT IS GONNA LEAVE
BUT I KEPT MY NEW STRUGGLES A **SECRET**...
FROM MY NEW FRIENDS, FROM MY **PARTNER**.
I JUST WANTED THEM TO **GO AWAY**.

AFTER AVOIDING THE SCALE FOR MONTHS, I STARTED WEIGHING MYSELF AGAIN.

IN A CHAOTIC AND UNFAMILIAR WORLD IT MADE ME FEEL **CALM** TO SEE THE NUMBER DROP A LITTLE OR EVEN STAY **STATIC**...

BUT IF THE NUMBER WENT **UP** AT ALL, MY HEART WOULD LEAP INTO MY THROAT.

I **KNEW** THE SCALE DIDN'T REALLY PROVIDE ANY RELIEF...

...BUT I ALSO KNEW I WASN'T HAPPY IN PHILLY, AND I DIDN'T KNOW HOW ELSE TO SOOTHE MYSELF.

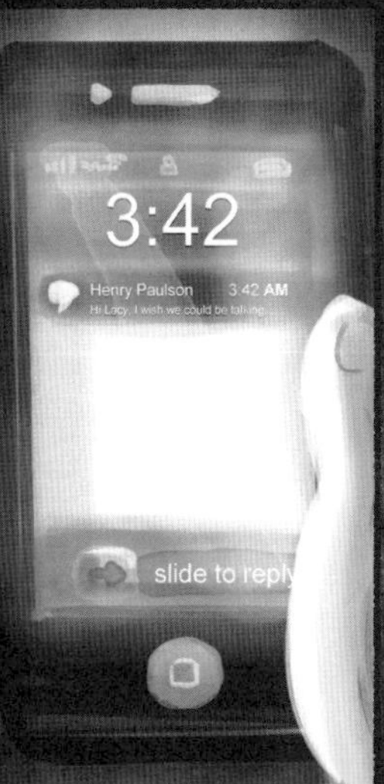

IT COULDN'T BE **GOOD.**

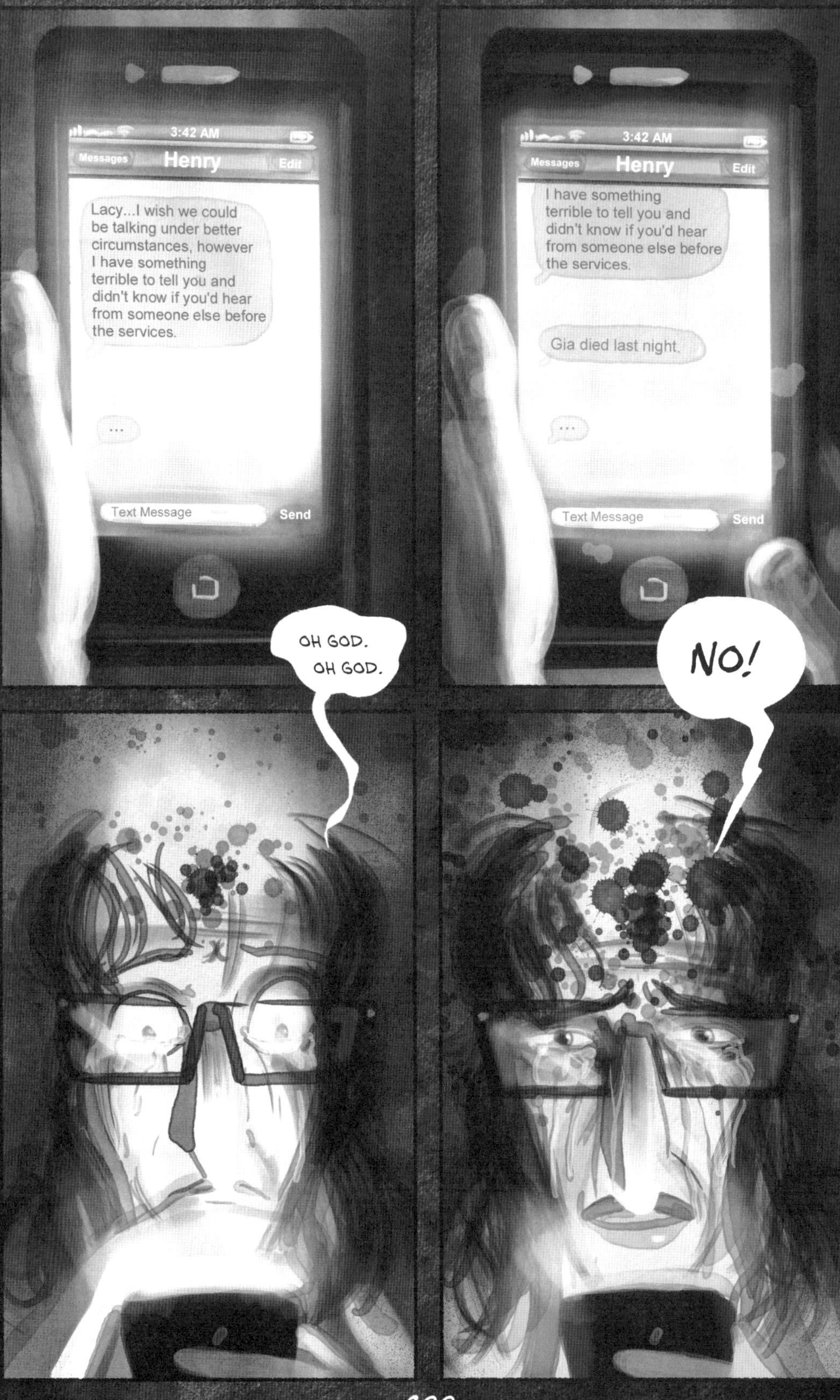
3:42 AM
Messages
Henry
Edit
Lacy...I wish we could be talking under better circumstances, however I have something terrible to tell you and didn't know if you'd hear from someone else before the services.
...
Text Message
Send
3:42 AM
Messages
Henry
Edit
I have something terrible to tell you and didn't know if you'd hear from someone else before the services.
Gia died last night.
...
Text Message
Send
OH GOD. OH GOD.
NO!

NO.
Messages
Henry
Edit
from someone else before the services.
Gia died last night.
At the moment that's all I know. I'm sorry.
Text Message
Send
NO.
3:43 AM
Messages
Henry
Edit
Gia died last night.
At the moment that's all I know. I'm sorry.
Text Message
Send
NO.
NONO NONO
NONONONO NONONONO NO
BABE, WHAT'S WRONG?
LACY?

HEY! YOU'RE SCARING ME!
TALK TO ME!
GIA DIED.
OH SHIT!
WHAT HAPPENED?
I DON'T KNOW.
I CAN'T BREATHE.

LACY?
HEY?
I NEED TO BE ALONE.
I'M HERE TO TALK...
I KNOW.
THANK YOU.
I'LL BE FINE.
I JUST NEED A MINUTE...
...TO CLEAR MY HEAD.
OK...

I NEEDED TO BE...
OUT OF SIGHT.
CLICK
LOCK
I NEEDED THE SPACE...
TO BREAK DOWN.

TO LET OUT EVERY DARK THOUGHT AND FEELING.
TO *PURGE.*
UP UNTIL THIS POINT *THROWING UP* HAD ONLY BEEN A PERIPHERAL PART OF MY EATING DISORDER.
BUT IT FELT **INSTANTLY FAMILIAR.**
FLUSH
HERE, ON THE OTHER SIDE OF STARVING MYSELF...
I HAD DISCOVERED A NEW WAY TO FEEL EMPTY.

AND LIKE INK
DROPPED INTO A
GLASS OF WATER,
THE URGE
SPREAD...

...UNTIL
EVERYTHING
WENT
DARK.

Chapter 10

I HAD THIRTY-SEVEN DAYS LEFT IN PHILLY BEFORE KETT AND I WERE HEADING BACK TO CALIFORNIA.

I PUKED MY WAY THROUGH THE CALENDAR.

LOSING GIA LEFT ME ZOMBIFIED.

I NO LONGER CARED IF I MISSED MY WORKOUTS.

I DIDN'T CARE ABOUT SEEING MY FRIENDS.

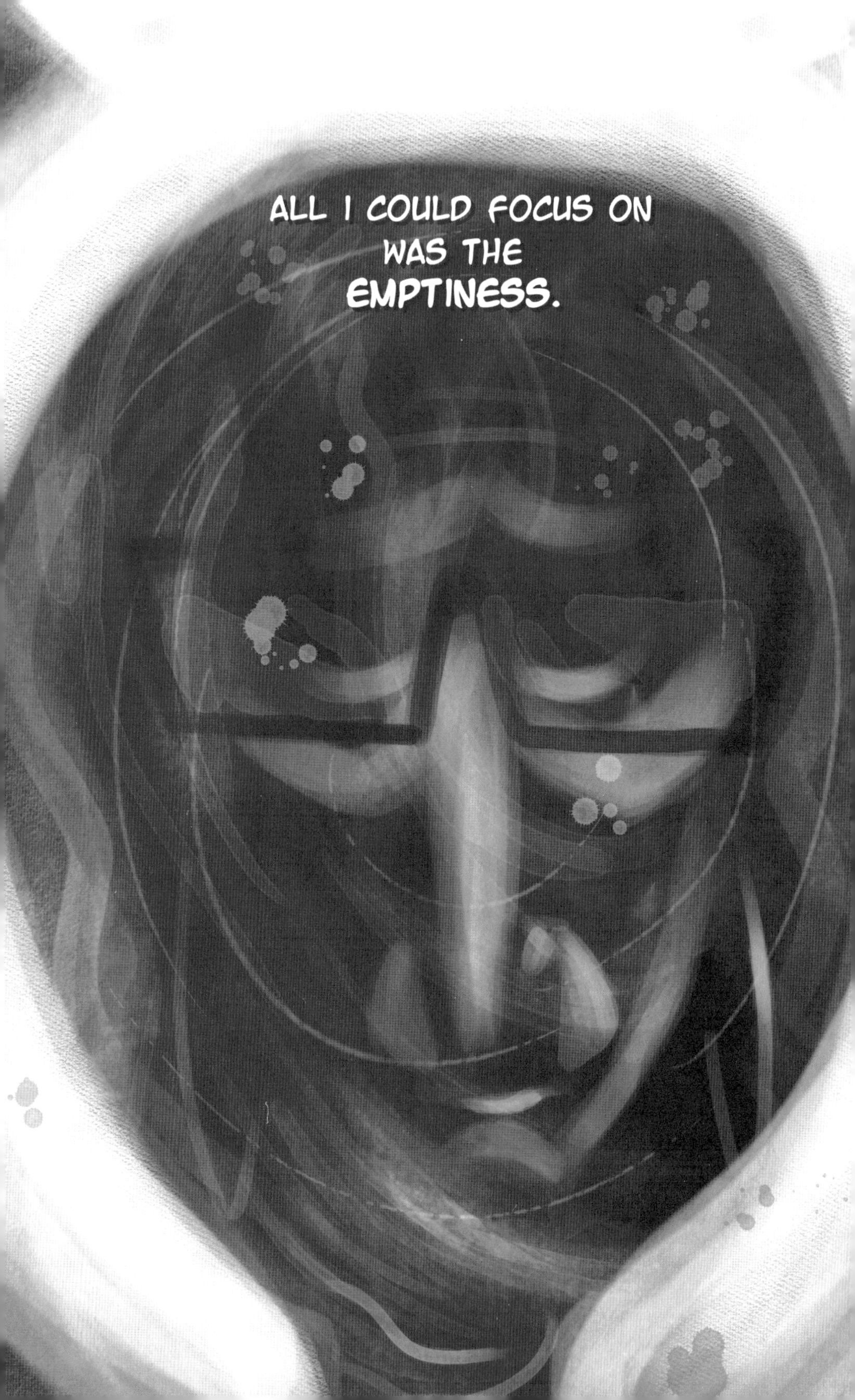
ALL I COULD FOCUS ON
WAS THE
EMPTINESS.

EMPTINESS...
FLUSH!
LIKE COUNTING CALORIES.

SCRUB
SCRUB
LIKE EXERCISE.

LIKE A MORNING PRAYER.
LOCK

FLOSS
ESSENTIAL FOR SURVIVAL.

I STILL HAD TO APPEAR TO FUNCTION NORMALLY.
RUMBLE

I KNOW.
I KNOW.
BLACK COFFEE.
I STILL NEEDED TO **WORK**.

I WAS BROKE.
THAT'LL BE $2.50.

SAME AS ALWAYS.
TOO BROKE TO FLY TO GIA'S MEMORIAL.

I NEEDED THE MONEY.

BUT WHEN IT CAME TO WORK...

I FLOATED THROUGH MY WORKWEEK.
AS THE DAYS PASSED, DETAILS OF GIA'S DEATH TRICKLED IN.
SHE'D BEEN PRESCRIBED STRONG PAIN MEDICATION AFTER SURGERY ON HER KNEE...
...PEOPLE DIDN'T BELIEVE SHE'D OD'D ON PURPOSE...
COME AGAIN.
BUT NEEDLES WERE INVOLVED.
THE DARKNESS OF GIA'S LAST DAYS WOULD GRADUALLY FILL ME UP.
COME BACK...

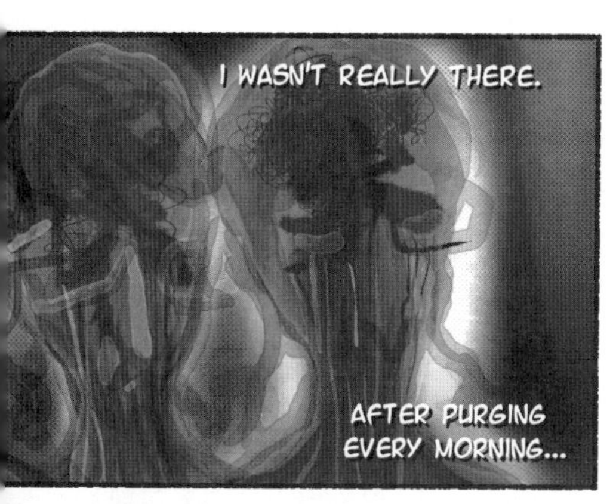
I WASN'T REALLY THERE.
AFTER PURGING EVERY MORNING...

I BECAME A GHOST.

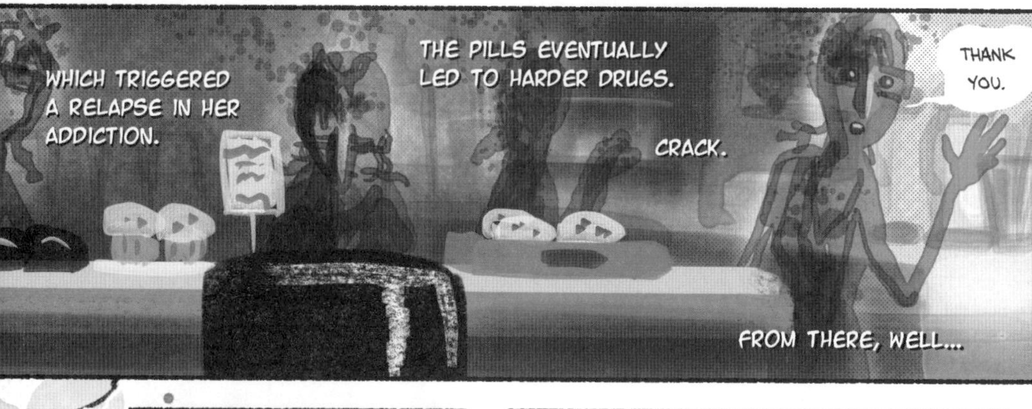
WHICH TRIGGERED A RELAPSE IN HER ADDICTION.
THE PILLS EVENTUALLY LED TO HARDER DRUGS.
CRACK.
THANK YOU.
FROM THERE, WELL...

UNTIL IT WAS TIME TO RETURN TO OUR SUBLET...

...ISOLATE...
LOCK

FLUSH
...AND EMPTY OUT AGAIN.

HEY BABE...

...WHAT ARE YOU DOING SITTING IN THE DARK?
NOTHING...

HOW ARE YOU HOLDING UP TODAY?
STRIKE ANYWHERE

CRINGE
WHOA.
SORRY...

NO, *I'M* SORRY, KETT.
IT'S NOT YOUR FAULT...

I'M JUST NOT FEELING GREAT.
I'M GONNA GO LAY DOWN.
'KAY...

LOCK

SOME DAYS I FELT LIKE MY RELAPSE WAS AN AWFUL SLIGHT TO HOW MUCH GIA HAD TRIED TO HELP MY RECOVERY.
SHE HAD WORKED SO HARD TO HELP ME, AND I WAS LETTING HER DOWN.

BUT AT OTHER TIMES I FELT LIKE SHE WAS THE ONE TO LET **ME** DOWN.

SHE TOLD ME THAT IF I JUST WORKED THE STEPS, THINGS WOULD GET BETTER...

THAT A LEAF COULD SAVE YOUR ASS IN A PINCH.

BUT THAT WAS BULLSHIT.

SHE'D GONE AND FUCKING DIED.

BEFORE SHE'D EVEN TRIED TO REACH OUT.

WHAT IS A FRIEND IF NOT SOMEONE TO CONFIDE IN?

LACY?
YOU **OK** IN THERE?

YEAH!
SPLASH
JUST FINISHING UP!

WOW.
YOU'VE BEEN SPENDING EVEN LONGER IN THE BATHROOM THAN ME LATELY.
I NEEDED TO SHOWER. I'VE BEEN FEELING SO GROSS.
IT'S COOL...

HEY, IF YOU NEED TO **TALK** ABOUT G—
NO!
KETT TRIED HIS BEST TO BE THERE FOR ME...

BUT JUST LIKE GIA, I WASN'T LETTING ANYONE IN.
I MEAN...NOT...
NOT NOW.
HEY.
I COULDN'T.

C'MERE.
IT NEVER EVEN OCCURRED TO ME THAT SHUTTING KETT OUT LIKE THAT...
I KNOW THIS SUCKS.
BUT IT'S GONNA BE OK...
...AND I'M HERE TO LISTEN IF—
I KNOW, BABE.

MAYBE LATER?
MAYBE.

...WAS THE SAME THING HENRY HAD DONE TO ME.

BUT KETT NEVER STOPPED TRYING TO BREAK DOWN THE WALLS.
SO, I'VE GOT A SURPRISE...
DO YOU KNOW WHAT FRIDAY IS?
IN FACT, HE FOUGHT EVEN HARDER TO GET THROUGH.
NO. WHY, IS THERE A NEW AVENGER MOVIE OUT OR SOMETHING?
NO, SILLY.
SOMETHING EVEN BETTER!
IT'S OUR OFFICIAL ONE-YEAR ANNIVERSARY.
OH SHIT!
KETT! WITH EVERYTHING GOING ON THIS WEEK, I—
DON'T WORRY...
I'VE GOT IT ALL PLANNED OUT!
YOU'VE JUST GOT TO TRUST ME!
IT TURNED OUT KETT HAD BEEN PLANNING AN EPIC NEW YORK CITY ADVENTURE TO HELP BRING ME OUT OF MY FUNK.
New York, NY
Long
1 h 14 min
1 h 49 min
King of Prussia
Philadelphia, PA
Wilmi
Newark
WE LOADED OUR BIKES ONTO THE INFAMOUS CHINATOWN BUS...
HOPE YOU GOT PLENTY OF SLEEP.
WE'VE GOT A LOT OF GROUND TO COVER.
WHOA!
...AND HIT THE STREETS OF NYC WHERE KETT HAD LIVED FOR MANY YEARS.

E HAD A TIME.
THIS IS MY FIRST TIME AT THE MET!
poor ugly happy
CENTRAL PARK
THE MET
WHEN I WAS SAD AND HOMESICK, KETT FOUND A WAY TO MAKE ME EXCITED TO EXPERIENCE SOMETHING NEW AND DIFFERENT.
BRYANT PARK
SQ
ABC NO RIO
CAKE SHOP
NOT ONLY THAT...
OOOH!
ALICE!
THIS IS MY FAV PARK IN THE CITY.
HE WAS SHARING HIS FAVORITE PLACES WITH ME.
AND EVEN THOUGH I HADN'T OPENED UP TO HIM ABOUT GIA—
PROMENADE
PROSPECT PARK
I HELPED PAINT THIS CAROUSEL BACK IN 2000...
COOL!
OR EVEN HINTED AT MY NEW BULIMIC BEHAVIORS—
HE COULD SEE THAT I NEEDED **CATHARSIS** FOR THE OBVIOUS GRIEF I WAS FEELING.
Aaah! Aaah!
YES!
Coney Island CYCLONE
AAAAAAAAAAAAAA!
CONEY ISLAND
HE KNEW I NEEDED TO ***SCREAM!***

WE SNACKED ON TASTY VEGAN TREATS THROUGHOUT THE DAY.

WE HIT ALL THE ESSENTIAL SPOTS.

FROM SCONES AND SOY LATTÉS...

WHERE TO NEXT?
YAFFA CAFÉ?

TO SALADS BIGGER THAN OUR HEADS.

KETT TREATED ME TO A ROMANTIC ALL-VEGAN ITALIAN DINNER AT **JOHN'S**...

AND WE FOLLOWED THAT UP WITH DOUBLE-SOY SCOOPS FROM **LULA'S**.

IT WAS ALL GOING SO WELL.

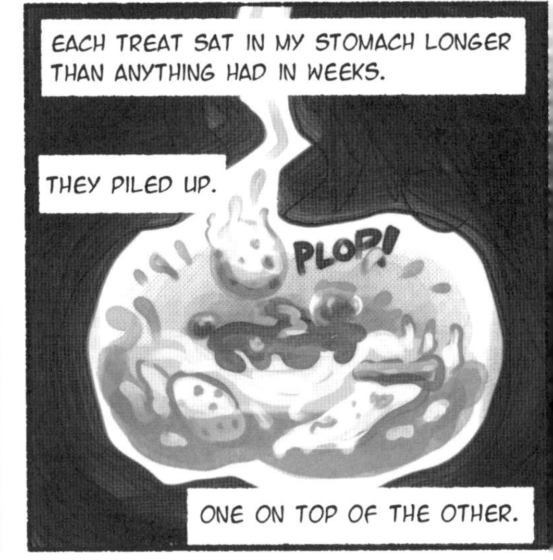

EACH TREAT SAT IN MY STOMACH LONGER THAN ANYTHING HAD IN WEEKS.
THEY PILED UP.
PLOP!
ONE ON TOP OF THE OTHER.

WE WERE JUST GRABBING ONE LAST COOKIE FOR THE ROAD.

FREE DELIVERY Atlas Cafe TEL
I JUST NEED TO PEE...
...THEN WE SPLIT?
SURE THING.

AND MAYBE IT WAS ONE TREAT TOO MANY...

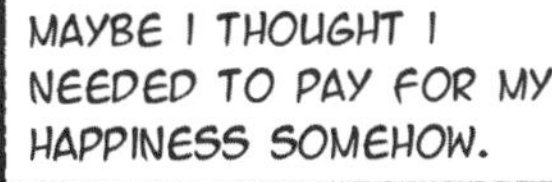
MAYBE I THOUGHT I NEEDED TO PAY FOR MY HAPPINESS SOMEHOW.

WHATEVER THE CASE...

I NEEDED TO PURGE.

ALL GOOD. LET'S BLOW THIS POP STAND.
HOLD UP.
AVAIL

I'VE GOT TO LIGHTEN THE LOAD NOW TOO...
BRB.
HA!
SEE YOU IN AN HOUR FREAK-A-LEEK.
poor ugly happy

THROWING UP HAD BECOME SO COMMONPLACE...

THAT GETTING CAUGHT NEVER EVEN CROSSED MY MIND.
HEY.
THAT WAS QUICK FOR YOU...
GOOD TO GO?

NO.
I'M NOT GOOD TO GO.
WHAT'S WRONG?
ARE YOU FEELING OK?

WHAT IS IT?

WHAT? DO I HAVE A BOOGER ON MY FACE OR SOMETHING?
SNIFF SNIFF
KETT...

YOU'RE **SCARING** ME.
NO...

YOU'RE SCARING ME.
WHAT?
WHY?
LACY...

DELIVERY
DID YOU MAKE YOURSELF **SICK** IN THERE?

I GUESS IT WAS ALWAYS ONLY A MATTER OF TIME.

BUT I STILL COULDN'T STAND TO BE CAUGHT RED-HANDED.

WHAT?

NO.

I DIDN'T...

I MEAN, I DID GET SICK, BUT I DIDN'T MAKE MYS—

KETT?
WHA?
WHERE ARE YOU GOING?
WAIT!

KETT!
IT'S NOT A BIG DEAL!
I'M OKAY!
COME ON! TALK TO ME!

YOU WON'T LIKE ANYTHING I HAVE TO SAY RIGHT NOW.
YOU WANT SOME REAL TALK?
FINE!
WHY WOULD YOU DO THAT?

I...
I DON'T KNOW!
IT... IT JUST HAPPENED.

I DON'T MEAN THE PUKING, LACY! I KNOW THAT SHIT IS A DISEASE!
I'M NOT STUPID.
THAT'S NOT WHY I'M PISSED.

WHY DID YOU LIE TO ME?

I'VE TRIED TO TALK TO YOU SO MANY TIMES AND GOTTEN SHUT OUT.
I CAN SEE YOU HURTING...
BUT YOU WON'T LET ME IN.

AND IF YOU WON'T LET ME IN...
THEN HOW AM I SUPPOSED TO HELP?

TODAY WAS SUPPOSED TO BE ABOUT CELEBRATING WHAT WE'VE GOT.
BUT IF YOU'RE GONNA KEEP SOMETHING THIS SERIOUS A **SECRET**...

...IF YOU'RE GOING TO **LIE** TO MY FACE...
...THEN WHAT KIND OF PARTNERSHIP IS THAT?
HOW IS THAT WORTH CELEBRATING?

I'M SO IN LOVE WITH YOU, AND I'VE BEEN CHEERING FOR YOUR RECOVERY SINCE YOU FIRST WROTE TO ME.
BUT?
IN THAT MOMENT I THOUGHT FOR SURE THAT I HAD LOST HIM.

BUT YOU CAN'T KEEP LYING TO ME. IF WE'RE TOGETHER...
YOU NEED TO **LET ME KNOW** WHEN YOU'RE STRUGGLING.

I CAN'T SIT ON THE SIDELINES AND WATCH YOU TREAT YOURSELF LIKE THIS.
YOU KNOW?
I KNOW.
I'M SORRY, KETT.
I KNOW I SCREWED UP.

I'LL DO BETTER.

THE BUS RIDE HOME WAS STRAINED.
PHILA
KETT...

KETT SLEPT, AND I THOUGHT ABOUT THE LAST FEW WEEKS.
...I KNOW YOU CAN'T HEAR ME.
BUT I WANT TO BE HERE WITH YOU...
HOW I'D LOST GIA AND THROWN MYSELF IN THE TRASH AS A RESULT.

IF I DIDN'T CHANGE, I FEARED I'D LOSE EVEN MORE.
I WANT TO LIVE.

...AND I'M WILLING TO DO WHATEVER IT TAKES.

I PROMISE.

Chapter 11

TWO WEEKS LATER, KETT AND I WERE BACK IN CALIFORNIA.

I STRUGGLED TO BREAK THE PATTERN THAT HAD EMERGED IN PHILLY.

MOSTLY, I SUCCEEDED.

SOMETIMES, DESPITE MY BEST EFFORTS, I DIDN'T.
I'D HEAR MY GRANDMOTHER'S VOICE TELLING ME TO GET UP OFF THE FLOOR...

AND NOW SHE WAS JOINED BY GIA.
ANOTHER GHOST IN MY EAR.
AND I'D **STAND UP.**

MY MEMORIES OF THEM WOULD PULL ME UP.

THIS WILL BE THE LAST TIME.

KETT AND I MOVED INTO A NEW GROUP HOUSE TOGETHER IN OAKLAND, AND CHRISTENED IT **THE RED CARPET**.
IT WAS A NEW HOME IN WHICH I HAD NEVER STARVED MYSELF.
A HOUSE I HAD NEVER THROWN UP IN.

MY OLD FRIENDS IN OA MIGHT HAVE ACCUSED ME OF PULLING ANOTHER *GEOGRAPHIC*.
BUT I DIDN'T CARE.
I NEEDED A CLEAN SLATE.

THINGS WITH KETT WERE TENSE.
GOOD TO GO?
YEAH.
GETTING CAUGHT WITH MY HEAD IN THE TOILET WAS THE SINGLE MOST HUMILIATING MOMENT OF MY **ED**.

HE WASN'T GIVING UP ON ME.
MUAH!
BUT I WAS SO ASHAMED.

I KNEW THAT IF I DIDN'T STOP PUKING, EVEN KETT WOULD EVENTUALLY HIT HIS LIMIT.

AND I SIMPLY WASN'T GOING TO LET MY ED COST ME THIS RELATIONSHIP.

THIS ONE WAS TOO IMPORTANT.

SO HOW WAS IT THIS MORNING?
UM...

SO EVEN THOUGH IT WAS SUPERHARD...

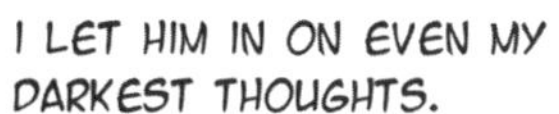

I LET HIM IN ON EVEN MY DARKEST THOUGHTS.

...PRETTY BAD ACTUALLY.

DID YOU THROW UP?

I DIDN'T WANT TO HIDE ANYMORE.

NO...
BUT IT WAS A CLOSE THING.

IF I WANTED TO GET BETTER, IF I WANTED TO PRESERVE MY RELATIONSHIP...

I REALLY WANTED TO, YOU KNOW?
WELL...
WHAT MADE YOU WANT TO TODAY?
YEAH?
I JUST FEEL SO GROSS! I HAD A SHITTY RUN THIS MORNING, HAD TO WALK HOME, AND WHEN I CHANGED...
MY JEANS DIDN'T FIT.

I HAD TO PUT IT ALL OUT THERE.

THAT'S OK. NEW JEANS ARE GETTABLE. I'M SORRY YOU HAD A HARD MORNING, THOUGH.
YOU KNOW, NEXT TIME YOU WANT TO PURGE, JUST COME TO ME BEFORE YOU GO TO THE BATHROOM.

OK.
BUT KETT?

...I MISS MY FRIEND.

WHY DID GIA HAVE TO DIE?
I DON'T KNOW, DOODLE. ADDICTION REALLY SUCKS.

IT'S OK TO JUST LET YOURSELF BE SAD.
IT WON'T HELP TO PUNISH YOURSELF.
I KNOW...

I JUST WISH I COULD DO SOMETHING THAT MADE ME FEEL BETTER!
I NEVER KNOW WHAT TO DO BESIDES **WORK OUT**!

MAYBE YOU JUST NEED TO *SWITCH UP* WHAT YOU DO FOR EXERCISE?

'CAUSE WHAT YOU'VE BEEN DOING JUST SEEMS TO MAKE YOU FEEL WORSE.

BUT WHAT ELSE CAN I DO?
I RUN. I RIDE MY BIKE.
WE DO "INSANITY."

THERE'S NO WAY I WANT TO GO BACK TO THE ELLIPTICAL.
WELL, I DIDN'T SAY TO DO *THAT*.
WHAT THEN???

I DUNNO, LACE.
I JUST THINK YOU SHOULD TRY SOMETHING...*ANYTHING* DIFFERENT.

"SOMETHING DIFFERENT."
Poogle
oakland/berkeley fitness
AN INTERWEB SEARCH FOR FITNESS OPTIONS IN THE BAY AREA TURNED UP ONE OVERWHELMING RESULT...

CROSSFIT?
I REMEMBERED HOW JAZZED RAMSEY HAD BEEN ON WEIGHT LIFTING BACK IN PHILLY.

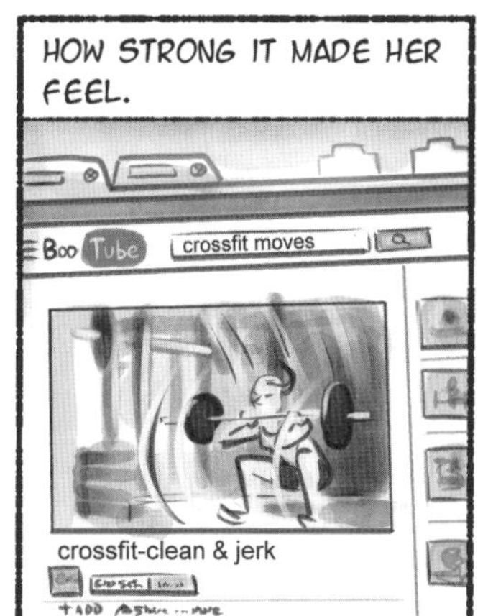
HOW STRONG IT MADE HER FEEL.
BooTube
crossfit moves
crossfit-clean & jerk
THE FEMALE CROSSFITTERS I SEARCHED FOR ONLINE CERTAINLY LOOKED STRONG...

BUT BIG.

WAY BIGGER THAN ANY SORT OF BODY I HAD EVER IMAGINED FOR MYSELF.

THESE ATHLETES LOOKED LIKE NOTHING I HAD EVER SEEN.
MANY OF THEM HAD BIG BUTTS AND THICK THIGHS...

BUT LOOKING AT THEM, I DIDN'T THINK THEY LOOKED "TOO BIG."
I MEAN, HONESTLY, THEY LOOKED FREAKIN' AMAZING.

WOW!
AS MUCH AS THE IDEA OF A BIGGER BODY STILL FREAKED ME OUT...I WAS INTRIGUED.

OVER THE NEXT FEW DAYS I SPENT A LOT OF TIME WATCHING LADY OLYMPIC LIFTERS ON THE INTERNET.
LOOK AT THIS ONE.
NEAT.
IT'S CALLED A "CURTIS P."

I THINK THIS KINDA THING COULD BE REALLY GOOD FOR YOU, LACE...
A WAY TO FEEL FIT WITHOUT FOCUSING ON GETTING SMALLER...
YOU SHOULD TOTALLY TRY IT!

I SPENT SO MUCH TIME WATCHING THESE STRONG WOMEN...
Poogle
crossfit gym woman coach
Search
TIP
TAP
TAP
TAP
TIP
I HAD TO AT LEAST TRY...

...TO MEET ONE.
oogle
rossfit gym woman coach.
Search
CLICK!

I NEEDED TO FLIP THE SCRIPT.

CHANGE MY PARADIGM.

BE COACHABLE.
GRASSROOTS
CrossFit
THAT IS...

TRUST IN A DIFFERENT MESSAGE OF WHAT FITNESS COULD LOOK LIKE.

HOWEVER CHALLENGING.
SHOULDERS BACK...

HOWEVER IMPERFECT.
TAKE A BREATH...

AND HOWEVER LONG IT TOOK
NOW STAND IT UP!
HRR!

IT WAS TIME TO FIGURE OUT HOW TO BE STRONG.
CONGRATULATIONS! YOU JUST COMPLETED YOUR FIRST DEADLIFT!
WOW!
SET YOUR BAR DOWN.
AND MELISSA WAS THE WOMAN TO SHOW ME HOW.
THAT WAS GOOD!
NOW WATCH ME AS I GO THROUGH THE NEXT MOVEMENT.
OKAY.
FIRST, WE RESET OUR POSITION AT THE BOTTOM.
HIPS BACK.
KNEES APART.
SHOULDERS BACK.

THIS MOVEMENT IS CALLED A "SNATCH."
WE'RE GOING TO CATCH THE WEIGHT OVER OUR HEAD...
SO WE NEED TO WIDEN OUR GRIP ON THE BAR.
THEN TAKE A BREATH...

AND **EXPLODE UP!**
?
KEEPING THE WEIGHT CLOSE TO YOUR BODY.

AND DROP **UNDER THE BAR**, CATCHING THE WEIGHT AT THE **BOTTOM** OF THE SQUAT.
I...
ARMS LOCKED.
I'M SCARED I CAN'T DO THAT.

* WORKOUT OF THE DAY

TWELVE MINUTES AND THIRTY-SIX SECONDS LATER...I WAS DONE. VERY...**VERY**...**DONE**.
HUFF
STILL, I FOUND MYSELF THINKING:
ONLY TWELVE MINUTES?
HUFF
PUFF
DESPITE HOW HARD I HAD WORKED IN THOSE TWELVE MINUTES, A VOICE INSIDE WAS TELLING ME I DIDN'T DO ENOUGH, HOW I WOULD NEED TO DO **MORE CARDIO** TO HAVE A *"REAL"* WORKOUT.

BUT THAT WASN'T THE VOICE I WAS PAYING TO LISTEN TO.
HOW WAS THAT?
-GASP- IT WAS... -PANT-...OK.
GO EASY THE REST OF THE DAY.
AND BE SURE TO EAT A **BIG MEAL** WHEN YOU GET HOME—LOTS OF PROTEIN AND CARBS.

YOU'LL NEED IT TO RECOVER. IT TAKES TIME TO BUILD STRENGTH. YOU NEED TO BE **CONSISTENT** AND YOU NEED TO **EAT** TO FUEL YOUR LIFTS!
BE COACHABLE.
OK.
I KNOW IT'S HARD WORK...

BUT **ROME** WASN'T BUILT IN A DAY, AM I RIGHT?
...YEAH.

SO WILL I SEE YOU TOMORROW?
UM.
SURE?

I WANTED TO COME BACK, BUT I WASN'T SURE I COULD MAKE THE LEAP MELISSA WANTED.

BIG MEALS? *LOTS* OF CARBS?
I MEAN, YES.
I'LL SEE YOU TOMORROW.
I THINK.
THAT NIGHT, AFTER WOBBLING HOME ON POST-**WOD** JELLY LEGS...

I HAD A DREAM.

I WAS BACK IN THE GYM WITH MY BARBELL.
BUT SOMETHING WAS DIFFERENT.
I WAS LIKE THE TIN MAN...
...ALL STIFF AND RICKETY. EVEN THE SLIGHTEST MOVEMENT HURT.
TICK
TOCK
TICK
INSTEAD OF A HEART, I HAD A CLOCK AROUND MY NECK. AND INSTEAD OF KEEPING THE TIME...
IT WAS COUNTING DOWN LIKE A BOMB.
TICK
I WAS RUNNING OUT OF TIME...
AND I NEEDED TO BE STRONG.
TICK!
TOCK!
TICK!
NO MATTER HOW MUCH MY BODY RESISTED, NO MATTER IF MY LIMBS GROANED OR MY JOINTS POPPED.
BRINNG!

IT FELT LIKE I MIGHT **BREAK APART** FROM THE EFFORT.
TOOOOOT
THEN A FUNNY THING HAPPENED.
I DID!

UNDERNEATH ALL THAT PAIN WAS ANOTHER ME...

...A **STRONGER** ME WHO COULD **SNATCH** WITH EASE!

A **BIGGER** ME!

BUT FOR THE FIRST TIME THIS WASN'T A SAD THING. IT WASN'T A COMPROMISE I MADE TO BE "RECOVERED." IT WAS SOMETHING I **CRAVED**.

IT WAS THE FIRST MOMENT I **WANTED** MY BODY TO **GROW** INSTEAD OF DISAPPEAR.

I SHOWED UP TO GRASSROOTS EVERY DAY...

AND PUSH!

DETERMINED TO MOVE THROUGH WORKOUTS THAT REQUIRED MENTAL FOCUS AND GRACE.

EVEN WHEN THEY DIDN'T COME EASY.

HOLY SHIT!
THUD!

WELL, THAT WAS BRUTAL...
BUT FUN!
YUP.

MELISSA AND HER PARTNER, KRIS, HAD A RELATIONSHIP WITH FOOD I HAD NEVER SEEN BEFORE.

THEY TALKED ABOUT EATING FOOD—EVEN **HIGH-CALORIE** FATTY FOODS—WITH ***EXCITEMENT***.

ONE DAY I SHOWED UP EARLY FOR CLASS. MELISSA HAD JUST FINISHED HER WOD.
YUM.
MY BODY IS TELLING ME IT'S TIME TO EAT ALL THE FOOD!

WELL, YOU DID GO PRETTY HEAVY ON YOUR LIFTS.
HI LACY.
HEY GUYS.
SO I HAD A QUESTION...
SHOOT!

DON'T YOU EVER WORRY ABOUT, YOU KNOW...
GAINING WEIGHT?

HMMMN.
NO.
NOT REALLY.

WE DON'T TEND TO STRESS ABOUT THAT STUFF.
WE KNOW WE NEED TO EAT TO FUEL OUR MUSCLES.
YEAH, AND A LOT OF THE TIME...

WE'RE TRYING TO GAIN WEIGHT.
REALLY?
WHY?

MUSCLES WEIGH A LOT!
AND STRENGTH COMES FROM MUSCLE.
MY EXPERIENCE IS THAT WEIGHT ON THE SCALE MEANS VERY LITTLE WHEN IT COMES TO HEALTH.

TECHNICALLY, I'M OVERWEIGHT...
AND I'VE NEVER BEEN STRONGER.
WHY? ARE YOU TRYING TO CUT DOWN?

OK, SO...
THIS ISN'T A BIG DEAL OR ANYTHING...
BUT I'M ACTUALLY IN RECOVERY FOR AN EATING DISORDER.
I'M STILL TRYING TO GET A HANDLE ON FOOD STUFF.

AND EXERCISE CAN BE SCREWY FOR ME TOO. SORRY IF THIS IS TMI.
I JUST WANT TO BE TOTALLY REAL WITH YOU GUYS ABOUT WHERE I'M AT.

THANKS FOR TELLING US, LACY.
I WILL SAY THIS, YOU DON'T NEED TO FOCUS ON WEIGHT LOSS HERE.
AND PLEASE LET US KNOW IF THERE'S ANYTHING WE CAN DO TO HELP.

HONESTLY, YOU GUYS HAVE ALREADY HELPED SO MUCH. I JUST NEED TO KNOW, LIKE...

HOW OFTEN SHOULD I BE DOING THIS?
'CAUSE, THE WORKOUTS TAKE A LOT LESS TIME THAN I'M USED TO.

WELL, LET ME ASK YOU THIS..
ARE YOU SORE TODAY?
WELL... ONLY WHEN I SIT DOWN...

OR STAND UP.
OR CLIMB STAIRS...
OR...

I GUESS THE ANSWER IS JUST YES!
AND WHEN WAS YOUR LAST FULL REST DAY OF ZERO EXERCISE?
MAYBE... *EIGHT DAYS* AGO?

WELL, YOU ARE WAY OVERDUE FOR A BREAK!
YEAH, LACY. YOU NEED TO REST TO GET STRONGER! RESTING IS WHEN YOUR BODY **BUILDS MUSCLE**!
GO HOME AND CHILL. NO LIFTING TODAY. **COACHES' ORDERS**!

SO INSTEAD OF WORKING OUT THAT DAY I WENT HOME TO STRETCH...

TO TAKE A NAP...

AND TO EAT WITH THE INTENTION OF BUILDING STRENGTH.

I KEPT LIFTING BUT ALLOWED MYSELF TIME TO REST AND RECOVER.

THIS CHANGED MY RELATIONSHIP WITH FOOD.

RESTRICTING MY FOOD OR THROWING UP WASN'T AN OPTION IF I WAS TRYING TO **BUILD MUSCLE.**

GULP GULP
LACE? ARE YOU EATING MY PEANUT BUTTER?
MUNCH MUNCH
UM...
PEANUT BUTTER
...NO.

EVERY TIME IT EVEN CROSSED MY MIND TO EAT LESS, I MADE MYSELF FOCUS ON THAT.

IF I COULDN'T EAT...
SHOULDERS SET BACK.
CORE TIGHT.
INHALE
DEEP BREATH IN...

AND **STAND.**
PHEW
BREATHE OUT!
I COULDN'T **LIFT.**

IF I DIDN'T EAT...
SLIGHT BEND IN THE KNEES.
HINGE AT THE WAIST.
DEEP BREATH.

EXPLODE UP!
FAST ELBOWS!
LAND IN A HALF SQUAT.
I COULDN'T GET **STRONGER**.

RESET.
GET YOUR BREATH.
SLIGHT BEND IN THE KNEES.
IF I DIDN'T EAT **MORE** AND MORE **OFTEN**...

PUSH UP!
DROP UNDER BAR!
LOCK ARMS!
...TO FUEL MY LIFTS...

AND STAND IT UP!
...I'D NEVER BECOME THE BUFF VEGAN FEMINIST WARRIOR I'D DREAMED OF BECOMING.

I **LOVED** LIFTING.
I LOVED FEELING STRONG.
AND GETTING EVER STRONGER.

...WITH LOTS OF HARD WORK,
PHEW!
THAT WAS FUN!
NOW TO CRUSH A POST-WORKOUT MEAL!

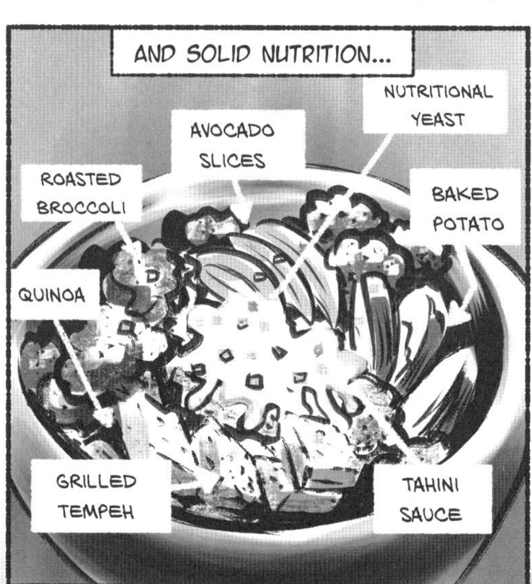

FLEX
...MY MUSCLES DID GROW.

AFTER A YEAR OF WEIGHT TRAINING, MY BODY DIDN'T AT ALL RESEMBLE THE SICK, UNDERWEIGHT GHOST OF A GIRL I HAD BEEN IN PORTLAND.

I LOOKED, WELL...

...KINDA **BUFF**.

KINDA SORTA LIKE THE PERSON I HAD ASPIRED TO BECOME.

WOW!

BUT I'M NOT GONNA LIE...

THERE WERE GROWING PAINS.
ARE MY THIGHS ALWAYS GONNA TOUCH?*

I WANTED TO LIFT MORE, BUT I DIDN'T ALWAYS LOVE THE CHANGES THAT CAME WITH IT.
C'MON!
GODDAMMIT!

FUCK!

WHOA!
WHAT'S WRONG?
LACY?

TALK TO ME, PLEASE!

NOTHING FITS, OK?
I'M HUGE!

NO, YOU'RE NOT!
I AM!
I'M SO GROSS, KETT.
HEY! STOP BEING A DICK TO MY GIRLFRIEND.

I JUST DON'T KNOW WHAT TO DO ANYMORE.
I CHANGED SO MUCH, BUT I'M STILL NOT BETTER!
RVIVR
HEY, COME HERE.

* ANSWER: YES.

I DON'T GET IT, KETT.
I DON'T THROW UP ANYMORE.
I EAT BIGGER, HEALTHIER MEALS THAN I EVER HAVE BEFORE.

I STILL WORK OUT...
BUT I ALWAYS MAKE MYSELF TAKE TIME TO REST AND RECOVER.

IT'S LIKE... NOW I'M DOING EVERYTHING RIGHT.
TAP TAP
I SHOULD REALLY BE BETTER.
BUT UP HERE?

I'M STILL FUCKED UP.
I COULD BE HAVING A GREAT DAY...

BUT THEN I'LL STILL BE STRUCK BY THE THOUGHT THAT I'M NO GOOD...
THAT I'M TOO BIG.

I'M JUST SO TIRED OF IT, YOU KNOW?
I KNOW, LACE.
HERE, STAND UP.

THIS IS WHAT YOU LOOK LIKE.
THIS IS THE WOMAN I LOVE THE MOST.
YOU'RE **BEAUTIFUL**!
I'M SO PROUD OF HOW FAR YOU'VE COME...
BUT *ALL THIS*...
...YOUR BODY AND ALL THE ISSUES THAT COME FROM HAVING ONE...
SOME OF THAT STRUGGLE WILL PROBABLY BE AROUND **FOREVER**... FOR YOU AND EVERYONE ELSE WHO'S EVER FACED DOWN AN **ED**.
BUT WHAT ARE YOU GONNA *DO*?

FUCKING **QUIT?**

NO WAY!

I DIDN'T THINK SO.

DIDN'T QUIT.
WHOOSH
I KEPT WORKING.

SWING
POP
SOMETIMES THAT EFFORT WAS *OBVIOUS*...

OTHER TIMES IT WAS MORE SUBTLE.
I RESTED.
I MEDITATED.
I READ.
IN 2013 I DECIDED TO MAKE A MORE FORMAL STUDY OF NUTRITION.

I WANTED TO LEARN MORE TO HELP MYSELF AND HELP OTHERS.
I'D SPENT SO LONG THINKING ABOUT THESE ISSUES, MAYBE I COULD DIRECT THOSE THOUGHTS IN A POSITIVE WAY.

WHEN MY SELF-ESTEEM DID HIT A ROAD BUMP...
PANT PANT
HUFF
PANT
I TRIED NOT TO PANIC.

THESE THOUGHTS WERE A PART OF ME.
I COULDN'T CONTROL THAT THEY WOULD STILL POP UP...
PUFF

BUT I COULD CHOOSE NOT TO GET TRAPPED BY THEM.
SHAKE SHAKE
I WOULDN'T LET THE NEGATIVITY AND FAT PHOBIA FESTER N MY HEAD.

I'D LET IT OUT.
RECOVERY FEELS TOO BIG TO HANDLE TODAY.
NO WAY!
THE ONLY THING THAT'S "TOO BIG"...

...ARE YOUR MUSCLES!
LOOK AT THAT BICEP!
FLEX
TIME LESS

YOU'RE SUPER STRONG!
HMMMN...

SECRECY ABOUT MY ED HAD NEARLY TANKED MY RELATIONSHIP AND KEPT ME STUCK IN THE PITS.

DIDN'T WANT MY STRUGGLES WITH FOOD AND BODY MAGE TO BE A SECRET FROM *ANYONE* ANYMORE.

I RECONNECTED WITH FRIENDS.

I OPENED UP ABOUT MY ED EXPERIENCE.

NO MORE BOTTLING UP MY FEELINGS.

MORE LOCKED DOORS.

BUT WHAT IF—
WHAT IF THERE WAS SOMETHING *MORE* I COULD DO?
WHAT IF...
WHAT IF I COULD TELL THE *WHOLE WORLD?*

TAP
TIP
TAP
TIP
TAP
TAP
TIP
GB

Epilogue

IN FEBRUARY OF 2013, **SUPER STRENGTH HEALTH** BECAME MY PLACE TO BRING RECOVERY OUT OF BASEMENT OA MEETINGS...

AND INTO THE **PUBLIC EYE.**

I WANT TO WRITE ABOUT **ALL** OF MY RECOVERY...
TIP
TIP TAP TAP
THE BAD STUFF...

AND THE GOOD STUFF TOO.
TIP TAP TAP TIP

WRITING ABOUT MY EATING DISORDER KEEPS ME ACCOUNTABLE NOT ONLY TO MYSELF, MY FRIENDS & MY PARTNER...
TAP
TAP
super strength health
blog
about
services
events
contact
BUT TO EVERYONE WHO FEELS LIKE LISTENING,

WHICH IRONICALLY MAKES ME FEEL THE **SUPPORT** OF EVERYONE TOO!

REAL TALK—
I DON'T THINK BEING RECOVERED IS POSSIBLE.
IT'S AN EVER-EVOLVING PROCESS...
NOT A DESTINATION.
THAT'S WHY I WILL ALWAYS CALL MYSELF A PERSON IN RECOVERY...
BECAUSE IT'S NOT OVER, AND IT NEVER WILL BE.
THOSE DARK THOUGHTS STILL OCCASIONALLY CRACKLE DEEP IN MY GRAY MATTER.
SOMETIMES THEY SPREAD.
BUT ONE THING I'VE LEARNED...

IS THAT HOPE SPREADS TOO.

CREATING A POSITIVE DIALOGUE FOR MYSELF...

BEING A FRIEND TO MYSELF...

plip

Plop!

PLOP!

Plip!

IS LIKE WATER IN INK.

PLip

IT DILUTES THE BULLSHIT AND WASHES IT AWAY.

OUR CULTURE DOESN'T ALWAYS SUPPORT LOVE AND RESPECT FOR OUR BODIES...
...BUT WE CAN'T DEPEND ON MAINSTREAM CULTURE TO GUIDE US.
SOMETIMES WE NEED TO TAKE THAT FIRST SCARY STEP INTO THE UNKNOWN.
pip
pip
plip
PLIP
PLOP

WE DO HAVE A CHOICE IN HOW WE TREAT OURSELVES.
I FOUND SOME HOPE.
AND THE HOPE YOU FIND MAY BE DIFFERENT FROM MINE...
BUT IF I CAN DO IT...
Plip
SPLASH!
PLIP

I BELIEVE YOU CAN TOO!
plip
pip
pip
PLip
LIP
plop
pip

(NEVER)

THE END.

PIP

plip

PLiP

Plop

PIP

PLOP

PLiP

HOW TO RECOVER FROM AN EATING DISORDER

A LOT OF PEOPLE AROUND YOU HAVE EATING DISORDERS. A LOT OF DIETS ARE EATING DISORDERS. A LOT OF PEOPLE WILL VALIDATE WEIGHT LOSS BECAUSE THEY LIVE IN A CULTURE OF EATING DISORDERS. IF YOU KNOW THAT, AND REALLY DISAGREE WITH THAT ON PRINCIPLE, YOU ARE A STEP CLOSER TO RECOVERING. CONGRATULATIONS.

IF YOU CAN FIND A WAY TO FILL YOUR TIME WITH THINGS YOU LOVE AND THAT INSPIRE YOU, YOU CAN EVENTUALLY BE OKAY. MAYBE YOU'RE OBSESSIVE, LIKE I WAS. MAYBE YOU SPEND YOUR TIME COUNTING CALORIES OR WATCHING THE NUMBER ON THE SCALE. THAT IS FUCKING BORING AND A WASTE OF YOUR BRAIN. FUNNEL THAT SHIT! KNIT OR SEW OR WRITE OR BECOME OBSESSED WITH SOME FORM OF CREATIVITY INSTEAD. YOU WILL HAVE MORE FOR YOUR EFFORTS, AND YOUR OBSESSION WITH CREATIVITY WILL NOT KILL YOU. USE THAT VOICE OF EVIL FOR GOOD.

GO OUTSIDE. THE WORLD IS FUCKING VAST, MY DUDES. THE SKY IS BEAUTIFUL AND WILL ENVELOP YOU; THE OCEAN WILL FREAK YOUR SHIT WITH ITS ENORMITY. LET YOURSELF BE SMALL IN COMPARISON TO HOW BIG THE WORLD IS AND KNOW THAT THAT'S ALL THE SMALL YOU NEED TO BE. IT DOESN'T MATTER HOW BIG YOU FEEL, THE SKY IS BIGGER.

BE SAD. LIKE, REALLY FUCKING SAD. JUST CRY A BUNCH AND THEN GET MAD AT HOW SOCIETAL PRESSURE IS MAKING YOU CRY. GET SO, SO MAD. LISTEN TO BIKINI KILL. MAYBE START A BAND AND FUNNEL ALL YOUR SAD AND MAD INTO IT. SAD AND MAD CAN BE GREAT. THEY HAVE POWER.

TELL EVERYONE ABOUT YOUR EATING DISORDER AND YOUR RECOVERY, BECAUSE SHAME KEEPS PEOPLE SICK AND BECAUSE THE WORLD NEEDS GOOD EXAMPLES. RECOVERING FROM AN EATING DISORDER IS THE HARDEST THING I HAVE EVER DONE, AND I WANT TO TELL EVERYONE ALL ABOUT IT. IT'S MORE IMPORTANT THAN MY MASTER'S DEGREE, MORE IMPORTANT THAN MY JOB. RECOVERING FROM AN EATING DISORDER IS MY PERSONAL MT. EVEREST. I DID IT, AND I WILL SHOUT IT FROM THE ROOFTOP. I DON'T PUKE ANYMORE, PEOPLE. GO ME!

MAKE FOOD AND EXERCISE CHOICES THAT YOU WOULD WANT LITTLE GIRLS TO MAKE. I LIFT HEAVY WEIGHTS AND, FOR ETHICAL REASONS (NOT WEIGHT LOSS REASONS), I EAT VEGAN. I WOULD TELL ANY LITTLE GIRL TO DO THE SAME, IF IT FELT RIGHT TO HER. I WOULD NEVER TELL A LITTLE GIRL TO EAT IN WAYS THAT LEAVE HER HUNGRY OR TO SPEND HOURS ON AN ELLIPTICAL MACHINE IF SHE DIDN'T LIKE TO DO THAT. I WOULDN'T TELL A GIRL THAT SHE NEEDS TO DO ANYTHING TO "MAKE UP FOR" FOODS SHE EATS. I WOULDN'T TELL A LITTLE GIRL TO THROW UP OR TO SAY TERRIBLE, MEAN THINGS TO HERSELF OR TO SKIP HER NEXT MEAL BECAUSE SHE ATE A CUPCAKE. I HUG THAT LITTLE GIRL, BECAUSE LITTLE GIRLS ARE FUCKING GOLDEN.

AND GUESS WHAT. YOU'RE GOLDEN TOO.

EVEN IF YOU HAVE EATING DISORDER BEHAVIORS FOREVER, YOU'RE PROBABLY STILL GREAT. JUST TRY ONE OR TWO OF THESE THINGS I SUGGEST. THEY MIGHT HELP YOU BE JUST A LITTLE GREATER.

PIP
PIP
PIP
DRIP
plop
Plip

Lacy J. Davis is a coach, public speaker, podcaster (*Flex Your Heart Radio* and *Adult Crash*), writer (superstrengthhealth.com), eating disorder recovery specialist, body love advocate, and artist. She has spoken about body image and eating disorder recovery for *Fit and Feminist*, *The Full Helping*, KATU Channel Two News, *AM Northwest*, *Driftwood Magazine*, and Vida Vegan Con.

Jim Kettner is a cartoonist, writer, illustrator, and podcaster (*Adult Crash* and *Galaktacus*). His work has been featured in *SF Weekly*, *Razorcake*, *Travel Portland*, *Driftwood Magazine*, and *As You Were: A Punk Comix Anthology*.

Both Davis and Kettner reside in Portland, OR.

Publisher's Note

This publication is designed to provide accurate and authoritative information in regard to the subject matter covered. It is sold with the understanding that the publisher is not engaged in rendering psychological, financial, legal, or other professional services. If expert assistance or counseling is needed, the services of a competent professional should be sought.

Grateful acknowledgment is made to Dischord Records for permission to reproduce the cover to Rites of Spring's self-titled album, and to Jody Bleyle for permission to reproduce the cover of Team Dresch's album Personal Best.

Distributed in Canada by Raincoast Books

New Harbinger Publications, Inc.
5674 Shattuck Avenue
Oakland, CA 94609
www.newharbinger.com

Cover design by Amy Shoup and Jim Kettner

Acquired by Ryan Buresh

Edited by Vicraj Gill

Library of Congress Cataloging-in-Publication Data

TK

19 18 17
10 9 8 7 6 5 4 3 2 1
First Printing

MORE BOOKS *from* NEW HARBINGER PUBLICATIONS

THE MINDFUL TWENTY-SOMETHING

Life Skills to Handle Stress… & Everything Else

ISBN: 978-1626254893 / US $16.95

WHEN PERFECT ISN'T GOOD ENOUGH, SECOND EDITION

Strategies for Coping with Perfectionism

ISBN: 978-1572245594 / US $18.95

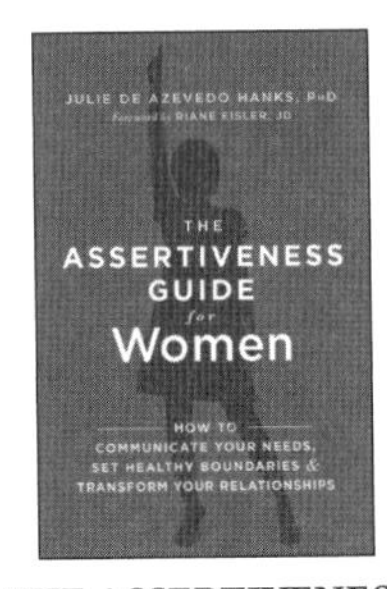

THE ASSERTIVENESS GUIDE FOR WOMEN

How to Communicate Your Needs, Set Healthy Boundaries & Transform Your Relationships

ISBN: 978-1626253377 / US $16.95

THE ANOREXIA RECOVERY SKILLS WORKBOOK

A Comprehensive Guide to Cope with Difficult Emotions, Embrace Self-Acceptance & Prevent Relapse

ISBN: 978-1626259348 / US $24.95

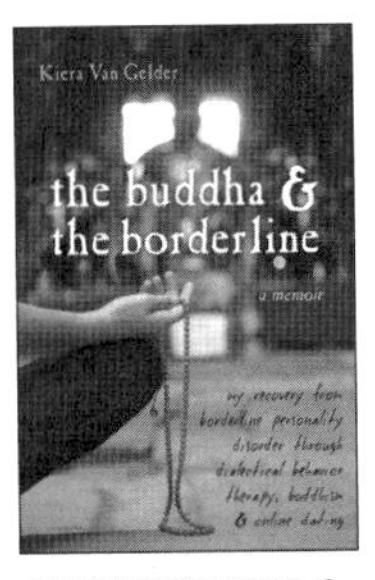

THE BUDDHA & THE BORDERLINE

My Recovery from Borderline Personality Disorder through Dialectical Behavior Therapy, Buddhism & Online Dating

ISBN: 978-1572247109 / US $17.95

THE LITTLE BOOK OF BIG CHANGE

The No-Willpower Approach to Breaking Any Habit

ISBN: 978-1626252301 / US $16.95

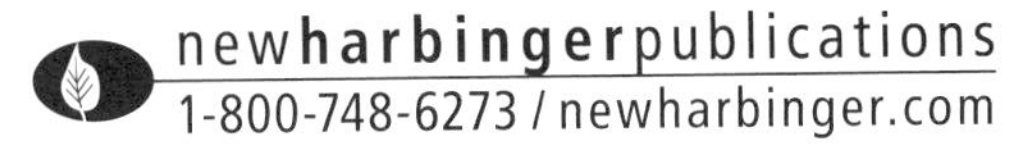

(VISA, MC, AMEX / prices subject to change without notice)

Follow Us

Don't miss out on new books in the subjects that interest you.
Sign up for our Book Alerts at **newharbinger.com/bookalerts**